About Island Press

Since 1984, the nonprofit Island Press has been stimulating, shaping, and communicating the ideas that are essential for solving environmental problems worldwide. With more than 800 titles in print and some 40 new releases each year, we are the nation's leading publisher on environmental issues. We identify innovative thinkers and emerging trends in the environmental field. We work with world-renowned experts and authors to develop cross-disciplinary solutions to environmental challenges.

Island Press designs and implements coordinated book publication campaigns in order to communicate our critical messages in print, in person, and online using the latest technologies, programs, and the media. Our goal: to reach targeted audiences—scientists, policymakers, environmental advocates, the media, and concerned citizens—who can and will take action to protect the plants and animals that enrich our world, the ecosystems we need to survive, the water we drink, and the air we breathe.

Island Press gratefully acknowledges the support of its work by the Agua Fund, Inc., The Margaret A. Cargill Foundation, Betsy and Jesse Fink Foundation, The William and Flora Hewlett Foundation, The Kresge Foundation, The Forrest and Frances Lattner Foundation, The Andrew W. Mellon Foundation, The Curtis and Edith Munson Foundation, The Overbrook Foundation, The David and Lucile Packard Foundation, The Summit Foundation, Trust for Architectural Easements, The Winslow Foundation, and other generous donors.

The opinions expressed in this book are those of the author(s) and do not necessarily reflect the views of our donors.

Stewardship of the Built Environment

Robert A. Young

Metropolitan Planning + Design
Series editors: Arthur C. Nelson and Reid Ewing

A collaboration between Island Press and the University of Utah's Department of City & Metropolitan Planning, this series provides a set of tools for students and professionals working to make our cities and metropolitan areas more sustainable, livable, prosperous, resilient, and equitable. As the world's population grows to nine billion by mid-century, the population of the US will rise to one-half billion. Along the way, the physical landscape will be transformed. Indeed, two-thirds of the built environment in the US at mid-century will be constructed between now and then, presenting a monumental opportunity to reshape the places we live. The *Metropolitan Planning + Design* series presents an integrated approach to addressing this challenge, involving the fields of planning, architecture, landscape architecture, urban design, public policy, environmental studies, geography, and civil and environmental engineering. The series draws from the expertise of some of the world's leading scholars in the field of metropolitan planning and design. Please see Islandpress.org/ Utah/ for more information.

Other books in the series:
The TDR Handbook, Arthur C. Nelson, Rick Pruetz, and
   Doug Woodruff (2011)
Planning as If People Matter, Marc Brenman and Thomas W.
   Sanchez (2012)

Forthcoming:
Reshaping Metropolitan America, Arthur C. Nelson
Good Urbanism, Nan Ellin

Stewardship of the Built Environment

Sustainability, Preservation, and Reuse

Robert A. Young

ISLANDPRESS

Washington | Covelo | London

ISLAND PRESS is a trademark of the Center for
Resource Economics.

Library of Congress Cataloging-in-Publication Data

Young, Robert A. (Robert Alton), 1931–
    Stewardship of the built environment : sustainability,
preservation, and reuse / Robert A. Young.
        p.   cm. — (Metropolitan planning + design)
    Includes bibliographical references and index.
    ISBN 978-1-61091-179-5 (cloth : alk. paper) — ISBN
1-61091-179-2 (cloth : alk. paper) — ISBN 978-1-61091-180-1
(pbk. : alk. paper) — ISBN 1-61091-180-6 (pbk. : alk. paper)
1. Urban renewal. 2. Public buildings—Remodeling for other
use. 3. Historic preservation. I. Title.
    HT170.Y68 2012
    307.3'416—dc23   2012014218

Printed using ElDoradoText
Text design by Paul Hotvedt
Typesetting by Blue Heron Typesetters
Printed on recycled, acid-free paper

Manufactured in the United States of America
10 9 8 7 6 5 4 3 2 1

Keywords: Carl Elefante, Christman Building, construction,
development, downtown revitalization, energy use, energy
utilization index, Fort Douglas, heritage conservation,
historic preservation, LEED, life cycle assessment,
National Register of Historic Places, National Trust for
Historic Preservation, passive thermal design, preservation,
rehabilitation, remodel, reuse, retrofit, smart codes, smart
growth, St. Louis Old Post Office, sustainability, tax credits,
United States Green Building Council

I dedicate this book to my late father,
Raymond W. Young,
who taught me more about sustainability than
either of us could have ever realized at the time.

Contents

Foreword

Each generation faces a changed and changing world. Even with the benefit of history's lessons, it is difficult to grasp patterns in the chaotic blur of events that rush past. It is an even greater challenge to know with any certainty which patterns signal the trends that define our times.

Today, there is nearly unanimous agreement that the defining pattern of the present is globalization. Worldwide economic, environmental, and cultural factors are interconnected in complex networks that resist comprehension.

The reach of the global economy is nearly inescapable. Investors are routinely required to exercise intestinal fortitude as the rise and fall of the Dow is pegged to events like the Greek debt crisis. While economies around the world still depend on the appetite of American consumers, Detroit automakers, rescued from the brink of bankruptcy, have garnered record profits largely from sales in the emerging markets of Brazil, China, and India.

Yet few have taken notice of a fundamental shift in global economic activity to a *restorative* mode, wherein the drive for expansion has been overtaken by the need to mitigate, adapt, and renew. Regarding the built environment, the shift has been far from subtle. Economic projections forecast that in the United States the value of building reuse and modernization will be double that of new construction over the next two decades.

In the context of this global shift to a restorative and sustainable economic mode, understanding what is of real and lasting value has the greatest importance. For those unfamiliar with the field, it may come as quite a revelation that the principles and disciplines of historic preservation hold the key. For those within the field, it may be an equivalent awakening to understand that the achievements of historic preservation have relevance in a much, much, wider world.

Over the past fifty years, the historic preservation field has defined a scalable model of sustainable economics. Historic preservation is founded on the principle that conservation comes first. Extending the useful service life of an existing building also extends the benefit derived from the investment of dollars, materials, and energy that went into its creation. Preservation activities tend to require relatively modest commitments of material and energy resources while demanding great skill and craft. Translated into the terminology of sustainable economics, historic preservation presents an ideal of steady jobs with good wages, cycles dollars through the local economy, and minimizes the depletion of resources. There is much to be learned from preservation economics.

The parallels between economic and environmental factors are apparent. By conserving what already exists, historic preservation improves the cost-benefit equation for past resource use and avoids expenditures in the present day. Curtailing the demand for material and energy resources reduces the environmental impact of constructing, maintaining, and operating buildings, towns, and cities.

Contributions of the building sector to resource depletion, environmental degradation, and greenhouse gas emissions are well documented. This data forms the foundation upon which the green building industry has been erected. However, even after more than a decade of concentrated effort to educate, advocate, and collaborate, the role of historic preservation in defining a sustainable future remains largely overlooked. From the perspective of historic preservation, the emerging pattern is clear. We cannot build our path to a sustainable future; we must conserve our way to it. The *greenest* building *really is* one that is already built!

From the outset, the international discourse on sustainable development focused in large part on its societal and cultural dimensions. Motivated by inequities between industrialized nations and those nations whose resources are exploited to stoke the engines of commerce, the principles of sustainability have been shaped by fairness and value viewed through the lens of culture. Despite this, social and cultural factors have been given short shrift in the building sector. The materiality of bricks and mortar seems to block out sensibilities needed to address the *softer* considerations of culture.

Historic preservation is the exception. To me, the greatest delight in practicing historic preservation architecture is that cultural value is placed on an equal footing with material value. Procedures for identifying and assessing historic and cultural significance are established as clearly as those for determining the integrity of building fabric. Proposed actions are judged in the context of actions taken in the past. Further, today's proposals are judged for their potential impact on the ability of future generations to establish their own connection with the legacy of past. The built environment is direct and primary evidence of past culture and, as such, is irreplaceable.

This book, *Stewardship of the Built Environment*, makes an important contribution to the literature about the intersection of historic preservation and sustainability. The stewardship of the built environment is simultaneously an act of preservation and sustainability. Stewardship is the core. Young explores the warp and woof of the rich tapestry of sustainable stewardship, illustrating both its vertical and its horizontal relationships.

By conserving what we have, today's investment of material and energy resources can produce meaningful economic benefit while helping to avert negative environmental consequences. Both elements are imperative. By appreciating the legacy of previous generations, we are challenged to understand the significance and value of our own actions in anticipation of generations and centuries to come.

Carl Elefante, FAIA

Preface

The road to the future leads through the past. Although many people in contemporary society perceive the goals of sustainability and historic preservation to be completely contrary to one another, quite the opposite is true. The past can teach many things that will help society get to a more sustainable future. Your choice to investigate this aspect of sustainable design already demonstrates that you have an innate curiosity beyond the prevalent perception that only new buildings can be sustainable. There are many myths and misperceptions about historic preservation and the reuse and rehabilitation of the built environment. This book guides you through the diverse aspects of reusing the built environment to uncover the underlying sustainability contributions and the often overlooked opportunities that building reuse and rehabilitation provides.

I am particularly excited to have this opportunity to expand the contemporary view of preservation and reuse as a sustainability strategy and am hopeful that a greater appreciation for the stewardship of the built environment will ensue. In teaching my classes, I often begin with a discussion of the use of the built environment as a personal living learning laboratory. Marcel Proust stated that "the voyage of discovery is not in seeking new landscapes but in having new eyes." This is a personal touchstone for how I have learned a great deal about sustainability and the built environment simply by observing how buildings work and the emotional and physical experiences they create. This skill has taken me far beyond a single book, classroom, or the Internet, to where I have learned how to read the built environment and understand the underlying principles and motivations for its construction, the builder's craft, the owner's intentions, and its societal importance of place.

This book provides an overview of the stewardship of the built environment (SBE) approach to sustainability and describes how preserving, rehabilitating, and reusing older and historic buildings contributes to sustainable design and respects the past, present, and future users of the built environment. Therefore, the talking points in any discussion about the SBE approach to sustainability embrace the following facts:

- Newly constructed office buildings or houses do not save energy immediately.
- Tearing down existing buildings and replacing them with new buildings that expand overall impacts on the ecosystem is a nonsustainable practice.
- The greenest building is one that is already built.
- Green sprawl poses an unseen threat to sustainability.

This book explores sustainable design through the use of the metaphor of three pillars to illustrate how sustainability is achieved. In this approach, the three pillars consist of social (S), economic (E), and environmental (E) factors that provide the common underpinnings for both historic preservation and sustainable design. It is commonly understood that each aspect of the SEE model must be equally considered or the process will become unstable and ultimately not fully achieve sustainability goals.

This book defines or illustrates the metrics that commonly are applied to sustainable design but with an eye toward the reuse of buildings both individually and in commercial and residential districts. In particular, the reader will learn how to read the built environment and pick out the precedents that led to the tenets of contemporary practices such as transit-oriented design, new urbanism, and smart growth. For individual buildings this will include an examination of how reusing an individual building can contribute to sustainability goals.

This book will give you a deeper insight into the retention and reuse of existing buildings and how you can use SBE to craft a more sustainable environment. After reading this book, you will be able to

- Use the essential terminology and metrics to identify the sustainable and historic aspects of existing buildings
- Interpret the social, environmental, and economic factors that contribute to the sustainability of preserving and reusing buildings (historically significant or otherwise)
- Recognize the sustainable aspects of buildings, neighborhoods, and commercial districts
- Differentiate between the regulatory processes that govern historic and older buildings

- Recognize the smart growth opportunities afforded through the preservation, reuse, and rehabilitation of buildings
- Identify sources for incentives that are available to promote preserving and reusing historic and older buildings

In the contemporary mindset that looks at new ways to construct the built environment (i.e., build society's way out of nonsustainable practices), often overlooked is the fact that preserving and reusing buildings can be a significant strategy in advancing sustainable growth goals. Growing evidence from successful projects fully demonstrates how preservation and reuse of existing buildings can be simultaneously socially, environmentally, and economically beneficial.

The book explores the overlooked opportunities for sustainability that reusing buildings can provide. You will gain a basic overview of the contexts that surround the reuse of buildings that have been designated as historically significant and those that are simply old. Although each designation is accompanied by a social status (or stigma), the opportunity for reuse is often dismissed early in the design development process due to a lack of awareness of what the positive sustainability attributes are or can become. The major focus areas for this book are as follows:

- *Energy use*: Not every old building is historic, much in the same manner that not every new building is more sustainable than all older buildings. A study by the Department of Energy revealed that the energy utilization index (EUI) for commercial buildings built before 1920 is lower than that of buildings built through the end of the twentieth century, and only the most recent buildings being built have comparable EUIs. Much of the public perception about existing buildings is based on the energy hogs that were built after World War II. Conversely, in the residential sector much can be done to improve energy performance and sustainability without tearing the building down. This is particularly true when we consider the energy consumed in demolishing a building and replacing it with a new building.
- *Energy recovery*: When a new "sustainable" house is built, it may take as long as 15 years to recover the new energy used to create the building materials, transport them to the job site, and fabricate the building. Tearing

down an existing residence and replacing it with a similar building will nearly double that recovery period because of the demolition and transport energy needed to remove the existing building and the embodied energy of the building itself. Similarly, a new office building may take as long as 40 years to recover the new energy used to construct it, and that period increases to 65 years when an existing building is demolished to make way for the new building.

- *Sustainable features*: Many buildings built before World War II already incorporate many of the "sustainable" features for which "innovative" buildings being designed and constructed today are winning awards. Among these, much study has been given recently to daylighting, thermal mass, and passive ventilation.

- *Resource recovery*: One of the examples illustrates that tearing down and replacing a residential building generates a material flow more than seven times greater than simply rehabilitating it. While the shift to a material reuse and recycle mode continues to gain favor, demolition still accounts for a significant proportion of landfill capacity. Similarly, the construction of completely new buildings accelerates the rate of extraction and depletion of raw materials used to make new building materials.

- *Historic guidelines*: The process for, advantages of, and constraints caused by the designation of historic status to buildings will be illustrated to dispel some of the more common misperceptions. Examples will illustrate that it is possible to qualify for historic preservation tax credits and earn Platinum, Gold, or Silver Leadership in Energy and Environmental Design certification.

- *Social and regulatory context*: Preservation and reuse occurs in areas of the built environment where people already live and work. Earlier successful efforts for preservation and reuse have been intermixed with a number of controversial issues such as the impact of urban renewal and interstate highway construction on local neighborhoods and business districts and their inhabitants. The oversight and regulatory environment can be daunting to those unfamiliar with the processes that have evolved. Issues of gentrification and displacement of residents have raised concerns about affordable housing. Trends in land use planning and development replicate features and amenities originally found in inner-city and first-tier suburban neighborhoods yet substantially occur at the suburban periphery.

- *Economic incentives*: In the contemporary economic climate, numerous incentives are available to increase the financial feasibility of preservation and reuse. Along with the Federal Historic Tax Credit program, two other major tax credit programs, New Market Tax Credits and Low Income Housing Tax Credits, are used to achieve significant relief from expenses associated with preserving and reusing buildings. Additionally, a variety of state programs and grant programs are used to assist in planning, designing, or constructing preservation and reuse projects.

The book is divided into five chapters that will help the reader understand what stewardship of the built environment can achieve.

Chapter 1: This chapter explores land use practices that have shaped the contemporary built environment and describes the role that preservation has played in society and the environmental movement. Because the reader may not have a preservation background, this chapter (and the remaining chapters) is geared toward raising awareness of the policies, procedures, and accepted practices common to the preservation and reuse projects that have been completed around the United States. This chapter also provides comparative insights into how preservation, sustainability, and land use are treated in other parts of the world.

Chapter 2: Building on the foundation of chapter 1, this chapter illustrates the social context, perceptions, and tools and processes that govern the preservation and adaptive use of buildings. Although the chapter focuses on the preservation and reuse of historic buildings, the insights given provide opportunities for emulating the preservation principles when working with non–historically significant buildings. Because of the broad nature of preservation practice, the points noted here are overviews to provide a general sense of the specific content.

Chapter 3: The environmental factors discussed here provide insights into how reusing buildings can be a sustainable practice. Moving beyond energy efficiency, the reader will see how such factors as embodied energy, energy utilization indices, and material flows can play an important role in the decision-making process. The reader will also learn what architectural form factors of older buildings contribute to their low-technology approach to increasing comfort.

Chapter 4: Economics drives every project. If a proposed project is viewed as economically feasible, then, if resources are available, it will get completed.

However, in the typically risk-averse domain of building construction, lenders, designers, contractors, public officials, and property owners need strong assurance that an unfamiliar process of adaptive use or preservation of an existing building is economically feasible.

Chapter 5: This chapter concludes the book with iconic case studies that exemplify the success of preservation and reuse nationwide, followed by a brief exploration of lessons learned and future implications and directions for stewardship of the built environment.

Appendix A provides a list of acronyms used in the book.

Appendix B provides suggested references for further reading, including relevant websites and a list of supplemental printed works that broaden the reach of the book.

In the digital version of this book, the reader can also click on the embedded hyperlinks throughout the book.

Acknowledgments

I thank the multitude of colleagues, friends, and family who have supported and encouraged my continued development of *Stewardship of the Built Environment*. In crafting this philosophy, I have listened to presentations by, read the writings of, and had discussions with a number of the leading preservation and reuse advocates that have greatly influenced my preparation for this book and my professional activities throughout my career. Among these advocates are Donovan Rypkema, Roberta Brandes Gratz, Stewart Brand, and Richard Moe, whose insights drive my continued engagement on this issue.

This work grew out of the closing chapter of my first book, *Historic Preservation Technology*, which discussed sustainable preservation and made me first see the need for a separate book on this topic. The catalyst for *Stewardship of the Built Environment* arose from an invitation by Robert Harden and David Woodcock of Texas A&M University to participate in a panel discussion at their 2009 Center for Heritage Conservation "Building on Green" Symposium. Preparing for that discussion led to the rudimentary presentation that has since coalesced into this book. While there, I was fortunate to engage Donovan Rypkema, Carl Elefante, Elaine Gallagher Adams, Ron Staley, and Gene Hopkins in a discussion that helped me clarify my perspective on how preserving and reusing buildings is sustainable.

A subsequent invitation by Jeffrey Chusid to speak at Cornell University's Preservation Short Course 2 further clarified my view of the potentially broader impact of this work. As I sorted out how to make it a viable publication, at the suggestion of Ryan Smith at the University of Utah I submitted it as an online course for a certificate program on sustainability at the University of Tennessee. I was further encouraged by Mark Dekay of the University of Tennessee to use it as the foundation for a book manuscript. After I developed the online course, Arthur C. Nelson, director of the University of Utah Metropolitan Research Center, urged me to submit it to Island Press, which has published it as you see here. I express my appreciation to Island Press for taking this on and particularly for the support I have received from Heather Boyer, Courtney

Lix, and the production staff who crafted the final work. I also thank the external reviewers whose comments enhanced my perspective on the manuscript.

My efforts have been further advanced by the support I received at the University of Utah from Prescott Muir, director of the School of Architecture; Brenda Scheer, dean of the College of Architecture and Planning; and colleagues Martha Bradley, Peter Atherton, and Patrick Tripeny.

I thank Jack Livingood at Big D Construction for granting me and my students ready access to the interior of their LEED Gold headquarters building in Salt Lake City, Utah. I also thank the Christman Company for their cooperation in providing photographs of their LEED Triple Platinum headquarters in Lansing, Michigan.

I include here my thanks for the support and insights I have gained from my Association for Preservation Technology colleagues, who form the core of my professional network. In addition to the aforementioned David Woodcock, Carl Elefante, Ron Staley, and Jeff Chusid, I thank Jean Carroon, Lisa Howe, Ilene Tyler, Mike Jackson, Jonathon Spodek, Fran Gale, Michael Tomlan, Andy Farrell, Hugh Miller, Ron Anthony, Anne Sullivan, Jill Gotthelf, Walter Sedovic, Patrick Sparks, John Lesak, Rick Ortega, and Dan Worth.

Most of all, I thank Deborah Young, my wife and lifelong companion, whose love, support, and motivation continue to propel me in new directions and into new adventures.

Robert A. Young
Salt Lake City, Utah

CHAPTER ONE

Overview and Introduction

Two quotations seem apt for introducing *Stewardship of the Built Environment*, an approach emphasizing reuse and preservation of our existing building stock. The first, "problems cannot be solved with the same level of awareness that created them," by Albert Einstein, encourages examination of an underused path to seeking solutions to sustainability. As we find ourselves on an increasingly resource-depleted planet with a changing climate, we *must* rethink how we build and develop. Many people have become so accustomed to creating new things that the idea of reusing or adapting something that already exists is new to them. In the particular instance of the built environment, however, the sustainable solution may not lie solely in creating new green buildings but rather in recognizing a new way of looking at the problem and seeking a potentially overlooked solution through retrofit, reuse, and preservation.

The second quotation is by Marcel Proust: "The real voyage of discovery consists not in seeking new landscapes, but in having new eyes." In this instance the new landscape literally and figuratively encompasses the increased sustainability of our built and natural environment. In reflecting on the meaning of these two quotes, the concept of stewardship of the built environment emerges as a valuable approach to increasing sustainability.

This chapter introduces the concept of stewardship of the built environment and provides an overview of how preserving and reusing buildings can be a viable strategy in crafting a sustainable built environment. It explains the antecedents that stewardship has drawn from the social, environmental, and economic contexts of the past and offers a look at the contemporary and future implications of pursuing this philosophy. Upon reading this chapter, you will have ample context for the detailed observations, arguments, and examples of stewardship of the built environment addressed in the rest of the book.

Stewardship of the Built Environment

Stewardship of the built environment is a philosophy (box 1.1) that balances the needs of contemporary society and its impact on the built environment with their ultimate effects on the natural environment (Young 2008a: 3). The goal of stewardship is to merge the reuse of the built environment with environmental conservation and to take advantage of innumerable opportunities that foster a more sustainable environment. Thus, this approach recognizes the value of reusing existing buildings to avoid the impacts that new building construction can create, both directly and indirectly, and also as a means to do the following:

- Decrease the long-term extraction and depletion of natural resources
- Abate the landfill pressures caused by the unnecessary demolition of buildings
- Reduce the consumption of energy used in demolition and the compounded effects of the embodied energy needed to create new or replacement buildings
- Reduce the creation of green sprawl
- Reduce the social, environmental, and economic costs associated with suburban expansion and land use intensification (fig. 1.1)

Conversely, stewardship of the built environment can foster long-term revitalization of the urban core by rehabilitating existing buildings to reestablish vibrancy in a community, district, or neighborhood. This vibrancy, which stems directly from a well-balanced approach to meeting the social, environmental, and economic concerns of the contemporary and expected demands of our population, is critical to the attainment of a sustainable society.

In the late twentieth century, a more holistic view of the impact of reusing buildings emerged from efforts to understand how existing buildings can go beyond the singular premise of energy efficiency and continue to contribute to the overall sustainability of the built environment. Most notable were the findings in *Our Common Future*, published by the World Commission on Environment and Development (WCED) and commonly referred to as the Brundtland Report, which concluded that sustainability is "development that meets the needs of the present without compromising the ability of

---

Box 1.1

Stewardship of the Built Environment Principles

Stewardship of the built environment recognizes that the preservation, rehabilitation, and reuse of existing older and historic buildings contributes to sustainable design; respects the past, present, and future users of the built environment; and balances the needs of contemporary society and its impact on the built environment with the ultimate effects on the natural environment.

The built environment is a subset of the overall environment and should symbiotically interact with the natural environment (i.e., what affects one will ultimately affect the other, either negatively or positively). Therefore, the guiding principles include the following:

- Sustainability is the integral and balanced combination of social, environmental, and economic forces.
- Reusing a building is the ultimate form of recycling. Demolishing a building increases landfill pressures and intensifies demands for new raw materials to create new building components.
- Preservation and reuse conserves existing social, environmental, and economic resources while revitalizing buildings, neighborhoods, and communities.
- Although retaining every building is not practicable, sensible efforts must be made to avoid unnecessary demolition or wasting of built resources.
- Accepting new land uses that preclude the preservation or reuse of the existing built environment, promote increased use of nonrenewable energy sources, or impose increased social, environmental, and infrastructural costs is inherently unsustainable.
- Beyond the footprint of a single building, ecological performance can be improved through land use strategies that complement the sustainability of a building or site at the local and regional level, such as public transit, bicycles, and walking, that reduce automobile dependency and the number of vehicle miles traveled using nonrenewable fuel sources.

---

future generations to meet their own needs" (WCED 1987: 43). Advocates for preserving and reusing buildings recognize that this approach complements sustainability efforts by demonstrating that the reuse of a building affects a broader view of the environment that extends into the effects on future generations. Preservation and reuse results in consumption of fewer resources than new construction and also helps moderate sprawl and its attendant negative impacts on social, environmental, and economic conditions.

Figure 1.1. Stewardship of the built environment considers contemporary and future needs of society and balances those needs with their impact on the natural environment. The philosophy recognizes that a critical part of that balance is reuse of the existing built environment to reduce growth pressures and their impact on the natural environment.

Stewardship of the built environment occurs as part of sustainable design where three factors—social (S), environmental (E), and economic (E)—optimally interact with one another. These factors comprise what are often called the three pillars of sustainable design, or the SEE approach to sustainable design. Stewardship of the built environment happens within this sustainable design region of the overlapping systems, taking into account the broader impact on the overall environment, in addition to the specifics of a single site or project.

The SEE approach, described herein, captures the singular definition of the Brundtland Report and broadens the perspectives of the social, environmental, and economic factors both separately and synergistically. Given the frequency of discussions about sustainability, the actual widespread adoption of a single descriptive phrase remains in flux; variations that describe sustainability in terms of "people, planet, and profit" (PPP), "ecology, ethics, and economics" (EEE) (Daly and Townsend 1993), and the "triple bottom line" (TBL) (Elkington 1998) are also in common use today. Although the exact words are different, they are essentially the same concepts.

Application of SEE to the Built Environment

The SEE approach can be a guide to improving the built environment by preserving and reusing existing buildings, redeveloping degraded sites, and building new infill construction instead of expanding the built environment with new construction in the suburban periphery. Development and growth that take place within the existing building stock—whether historic or simply old buildings—can mitigate further degradation of the local (and, in aggregate, the global) environment. The often overlooked crux of the matter is that construction of new "sustainable" buildings on the suburban periphery entails investment of significant energy resources, may contribute to increased air pollution via automobile-only access, and also may increase the societal costs of public infrastructure and cultural isolationism. Strictly adhering to a new-construction-only approach also has global implications because the use of new materials (i.e., no recycled content) has cumulative impacts on the social fabric, environmental integrity, and the economy as natural resources are extracted, processed, transported, and installed in the building.

Recycling metals, glass, paper, and plastics and the broad societal gains that recycling fosters have gained attention over the past decade. Let us for a moment consider that reusing a building is the ultimate form of the mantra "reduce, reuse, recycle." In recognizing stewardship of the built environment as a significantly larger-scale application of this simple holistic strategy, we can expect building preservation and reuse to have significant implications for reducing social, environmental, and economic pressures and thereby increasing sustainability along the entire spectrum of building design, construction, use, and operation. As a consequence, we need to take a more enlightened look at how we preserve and reuse our built environment by reinvesting in and retrofitting existing buildings to meet contemporary and future needs of society.

The philosophy of stewardship of the built environment draws from the recognition of these tenets:

- The greenest building is one that is already built (Elefante 2007: 26).
- Newly constructed buildings do not save energy immediately (Jackson 2005: 45–52).
- Demolishing existing buildings and replacing them with new buildings that increase overall ecological impacts is not sustainable (Young 2008b: 57–60).
- Recent quantification metrics and assessment systems provide a mechanism to evaluate overall sustainability (Campagna 2008: 1–2, 6).
- Sprawl, even green sprawl, is a threat to sustainability (Shapiro 2007).

The first statement here, that the greenest building is one that is already built, makes the point that money, energy, and material resource savings have often revealed that reuse of an existing building has a number of sustainable qualities that are overlooked in the continued perception that we can use new construction to build our way to sustainability.

Over the past few years, a more comprehensive look at the life cycle analysis of a building that includes nonenergy impacts such as carbon and water consumption has been gaining favor. In this approach, alternative choices are compared based on the avoided impacts of design choices. Several studies conducted by the Athena Sustainable Materials Institute in Canada have demonstrated that preservation and reuse of buildings often provides the most sustainable outcome of project options when compared with constructing a comparable new building.

One of the more complex issues to understand is that although newly constructed green buildings are designed to use less energy than those from the late twentieth century, *the overall process of constructing these new green buildings does not immediately save energy.* This is because no true energy savings accrue until the energy used to create the new building is recouped. So although a new building may consume energy at a lower rate than an existing building, it must overcome the energy deficit generated before it actually saves energy in comparison to reusing a building. The environmental impacts are further exacerbated when a building is demolished to make way for the new construction. As noted in *The Greenest Building: Quantifying the Environmental Value of Building Reuse,* "it can take between 10 and 80 years for a new energy-efficient building to overcome, through more efficient operations, the negative climate change impacts that were created during the construction process" (Preservation Green Lab 2012: iv). When existing buildings are replaced with new construction, energy deficits increase substantially because of the energy used in the demolition (and some will argue for recognition of the wasting of the embodied energy, water, and carbon used in the original construction of the building as well). Also, demolition debris increases pressure on landfills. With demolition debris accounting for nearly 40 percent of current landfill volumes, this impact is significant.

The construction industry has been steadily increasing the recycling of base materials with such programs as Habitat for Humanity's ReStore program (Habitat for Humanity 2012). However, until a component and material *reuse* industry develops that looks to comprehensively reuse building materials at their same level of use (e.g., salvaging) and moves beyond the current recycling approach that downcycles building materials (e.g., grinding up materials to be used as filler in other construction products), the practice of demolishing existing buildings and replacing them with new ones will remain an inherently nonsustainable enterprise. This is where the life cycle analysis approach plays an increasingly important role in determining the true sustainability of a building design and construction decision.

Concerns about misinformation and, perhaps, misrepresentation of sustainability (i.e., green-greenwashing) prompted the development and introduction of more comprehensive sustainability metric systems and assessment tools by the end of the twentieth century. The concept of energy efficiency was embraced by proponents of the environmental movement and eventually evolved into the current sustainability movement. While people, companies,

and organizations attempted to increase the sustainability of the built environment, competition in the market motivated some to engage in greenwashing
(e.g., to extol their qualities as green when in fact the validity of their claims
was suspect). As a result of this abuse, demand grew for a systematic way to
quantify how green or sustainable a building was when completed and eliminate greenwashing practices. Initially, the creators of these rating systems focused on what new construction could do to become more sustainable, and it
was not unexpected to see many quantification methods addressing primarily
new construction.

Although there are many quantification systems worldwide, the current
leading program in the United States is the US Green Building Council's
Leadership in Energy and Environmental Design (LEED) (USGBC 2010).
The LEED program includes many different categories in which a voluntary
rating can be earned, including LEED for new construction (NC), existing
buildings (EB), commercial interiors (CI), core & shell (CS), schools (SCH),
healthcare (HC), neighborhood design (ND), retail, and homes.

LEED measures how well a project conforms to best practices for a specific
array of core sustainability criteria that are divided into several assessment area
categories: sustainable sites, water efficiency, energy and atmosphere, materials and resources, indoor environmental quality, innovation and design process, and regional priority credits. The quantification process typically assigns
points or credits to these specific aspects of a project based on how well they
conform to the target values of the assessment system. Each of the assessment
areas has its own set of credits, and it is not necessary to earn every credit.
Instead, LEED assigns a Platinum, Gold, Silver, or Certified designation to a
building based on the total number of credits attained overall. Buildings may
achieve those designations based on substantially higher performance in the
non-energy-related categories.

Initial versions of LEED were decried by the preservation community because of the low level of recognition that reusing buildings as a sustainability
strategy received. For example, reusing a building merited the same value as
installing a bike rack: 1 point. LEED NC has since been refined to incorporate more sensitivity toward reusing buildings (Kienle 2008; Campagna 2008:
1–2, 6). LEED EB addresses upgrades to the operating systems of existing
buildings. Even with such an inauspicious beginning, the LEED program has
already recognized numerous projects that have reused existing historic buildings (fig. 1.2).

Figure 1.2. Before and after views of the Ecotrust Building in Portland, Oregon, which was the first historic restoration that earned a LEED-NC Gold rating (© Ecotrust, http://www.ecotrust.org, image used with permission).

As the rating systems and supporting methods have developed over the past decade, there has also been a growing realization that some buildings have not met the projected performance models used to determine their predicted level of sustainability. This indicates that there is still room for improving the overall approach to predicting future performance and assessing actual sustainability. These quantification systems have created another unintended consequence by initially focusing on only the building and the immediate site, to the exclusion of a broader planning-oriented view that includes sustainable transportation choices. Unlike large public works projects that require an environmental impact study (EIS), the site-at-hand approach has long been the norm for nearly all private construction activities. So, although programs such as LEED award points for projects that accommodate alternative forms of transportation (e.g., bicycles, transit), they do not necessarily penalize projects that do not. Over the past decade, building design, construction, and operation professionals have made significant strides in moving toward sustainable new buildings. Meanwhile, civic leaders have encouraged the development of new construction projects that include many of the sustainability aspects that are desirable at the community scale. However, in a free market economy, there are always unintended consequences. With the institutionalized reliance on the automobile and only a recent broadening of recognition of opportunities afforded by transit-oriented development, many of the more highly regarded sustainable projects that looked only at the onsite aspects of sustainability and not the larger built environment have fallen under criticism.

Unlike in Europe, where steep fuel taxes inhibit the use of the automobile (which concurrently curtails sprawl and encourages alternative forms of transportation), in the United States the significantly lower fuel tax system encourages not only sprawl but even more automobile usage without regard for the true increase in environmental costs attributed to vehicle miles traveled annually. Green buildings are appearing in locations where increased automobile dependence threatens to negate the efforts these projects make toward sustainability. Beyond misunderstandings about the inherent sustainability of reusing buildings, the emerging recognition that these rating programs have inspired "green sprawl" is just coming into public discussion. Shari Shapiro, author of the *Green Building Law Blog*, noted that

> Allowing a building to be certified "green" but built in an unsustainable context provides justification for continued sprawling development. Sprawling development has many adverse consequences, including air and water pollution, open space destruction, degradation of towns and cities, and increased need for infrastructure. (Shapiro 2007)

Thus, green sprawl is a growing concern that prompts criticism for any project that does not accommodate alternative forms of transportation to reduce the number of vehicle miles traveled and its attendant impacts on air pollution, community health and safety, and community infrastructure costs. The big-box retailer on the suburban periphery, even if constructed with the most sustainable prototypical building design, may jeopardize its sustainability gains when evaluated according to the SEE impacts of automobile transportation necessary to patronize the store. Even worse are the corporations that view their assets only in terms of a specific corporate identity that does not accommodate the reuse of existing buildings or insists on removing existing buildings to make way for new construction. In a growing number of communities, forward-thinking community leaders have maintained community development goals through sensitive building reuse and infill, especially in their central business districts. This steadfastness has enabled the reuse of buildings through retrofitting and rehabilitation strategies that respect the community's identity while increasing opportunities for reinvestment in the vitality of the community (fig. 1.3).

Although the term *green sprawl* is aimed at big-box retail buildings at the suburban periphery, this is also a blind spot for environmentalists seeking sustainability. For example, the Philip Merrill Environmental Center (completed in 2000) earned the first LEED-NC Platinum rating. However, the building site, constructed 10 miles from the original headquarters in downtown Annapolis, Maryland, has caused many of the one hundred employees to drive instead of walk to work. It is unknown how the increased fuel consumption (and the attendant impacts on air quality) for commuting might offset the energy savings from the new building (Curtis 2008). However, this raises the question as to whether constructing even a net zero energy building can contribute to sustainability if the transportation needs increase the vehicle miles traveled, the dependence on automobiles, and the health problems caused by increased air pollution (fig. 1.4).

Thinking beyond the site and understanding the impacts at the community and regional level still remains an elusive goal, albeit one very much in harmony with preservation and reuse of the existing built environment.

Social Contributions of Preservation and Reuse

Preserving and reusing buildings also helps retain a sense of social identity, community, and connectedness to place that has been increasingly absent in the commoditized built landscape. Older and historic buildings, created at a time when builders intended them to be used forever and often constructed with locally available materials and interesting details, are connected to the

Figure 1.3. This McDonald's restaurant in Freeport, Maine, which adaptively uses a Federal-era farmhouse, demonstrates that community leaders can retain a sense of place in their community and require that buildings be reused rather than be replaced.

Figure 1.4. A view of smog-filled Los Angeles as seen from the LEED Silver-rated Getty Museum. Could green sprawl negate the sustainability improvements of new buildings by increasing the vehicle miles traveled to get to them? Can Americans recognize the sustainable benefits of reusing and preserving the built environment?

character of place in a way that is often ignored in newer buildings. The mass replication of franchise architecture, suburban housing, and corporate office parks has created a less differentiated built environment nationwide that has contributed to a growing sense of placelessness.

In addition, older buildings are generally located in the heart of urban areas: downtowns and compact urban or first-ring suburban neighborhoods that are increasingly attractive places to live, for a variety of reasons. People are growing frustrated with suburban isolation, lack of transportation choices, increased sprawl, long commutes, increased air pollution, and higher living costs associated with living in (and expanding) the suburbs. Consequently, diverse populations are looking for greater social interaction and connectedness in attractive environments that do not rely solely on private automobile transportation. Empty-nesters are seeking housing that does not include large yards (with the attendant upkeep), and they look for connections to cultural activities and venues associated with existing urban cores. Concurrently, young professionals are attracted to shorter commutes and greater social connectedness that urban living provides (Nelson 2011).

Alternative forms of transportation such as bicycles, walking, and public transit are growing in popularity, and older buildings are often conveniently located in areas able to accommodate multimodal transportation options, unlike the suburbs. As Breen and Rigby noted in *Intown Living: A Different American Dream* (2004: 4), what people are seeking is *urbanism*, which translates into the built environment as walkability, density, diversity, hipness, and public transit. Preserving and reusing the built environment, especially in urban environments, can help meet these emerging market demands.

The term *historic preservation*, as applied to existing buildings, confuses many. In the United States, historic preservation is frequently and erroneously viewed as placing numerous restrictions on a building that may interfere with future uses. As stated by Donovan D. Rypkema, executive director of the Washington, DC consulting firm PlaceEconomics and a leading voice from the private sector in the efforts to promote building rehabilitation,

Sustainability means stewardship. Historic preservation is sustainable development.

Development without historic preservation is not sustainable. That's what your stewardship is assuring today, and future generations will thank you for it tomorrow. (Rypkema 2006)

Beyond a direct reduction in material and energy flows, stewardship related to historic preservation recognizes the importance of the cultural layering of historically significant aspects of earlier cycles of land development and how they affect and are affected by future development. Although not all existing buildings are historically significant, their rehabilitation and reuse can be part of a conservation ethic that seeks to understand not only the contribution they can make toward a more sustainable future but also how they affect social identity and connections to place.

Emergence of a Stewardship Ethos

To fully understand the social imperative for stewardship through the preservation and reuse of buildings, we must first comprehend the emergence of historic preservation practice and the changes in leaders' recognition of its importance as a sustainability strategy. In the United States, the term *historic preservation* is singularly used to describe four different treatment processes: preserving, rehabilitating, conserving, and reconstructing a building. It is therefore not surprising that many people are confused about the specific intent behind the historic preservation movement, how the profession is practiced, and how it contributes to social sustainability. Many who do not fully understand the broader implications of what historic preservation can foster view it simply as clinging to the past and standing in the way of progress. In Europe and Canada, the comparable term *heritage conservation* denotes a means of maintaining connections to cultural origins and celebrating cultural traditions.

This perception arose in the United States because many early historic preservation efforts connected with nostalgia and sentimental attachment, focused only on the best archetypical examples of a style, identified only buildings with specific associations with wealthy or historically significant people, or reused a building as a "house museum" that was frozen in time (fig. 1.5). These practices, coupled with the fact that wealthy people took the lead on these early efforts, also led many to see preservation as the purview of the rich. Vernacular landscapes of the everyday common person and the poorer, inner-city neighborhoods that consisted of a mix of lower socioeconomic constituencies with little political strength or voice were largely dismissed, and many eventually succumbed to urban renewal programs and interstate highway construction.

Figure 1.5. Restorations such as the Paul Revere House in Boston, Massachusetts are a direct example of the priorities of early preservationists, which led to a public perception that preservation was an avocation of the wealthy and was intended solely to make museums out of significant buildings.

Historic preservation thus suffers from the perceptual stigma of being antiprogressive, clinging unnecessarily to the past, and as being a hobby of the wealthy with no connection to the everyday man or woman. This lingering perception has formed a significant impediment to the broader acceptance of preservation (i.e., conservation) and reuse of existing buildings as is practiced in Europe, where the conservation of heritage and social identity is more strongly associated with reusing buildings and making them contribute to the vitality of the built environment.

Context of Stewardship: Historic Preservation and Adaptive Reuse in the United States

To more fully understand how preservation and reuse have been traditionally viewed in the United States, a little review is needed on the social contexts of the settlement of North America. Originally, the built environment of early European settlements in America was crafted to facilitate the extraction and transformation of raw materials into goods to be sold, house the population that fostered that transformation, and accommodate the societal constructs that fulfilled the spiritual, educational, cultural, recreational, and service needs of that population. The extraction and depletion approach to managing natural resources and the successive waves of migration and periods of economic prosperity and decline created changes in the built environment. Existing buildings were removed, and new buildings replaced them. Prosperity and decline created growth pressures as cities and towns became more urban, remained small, or lost population to more successful communities elsewhere. The economic imperative to have access to transportation (e.g., railroads), water, cheap land, and a better quality of life were significant factors determining whether settlements grew.

Cycles of prosperity and decline had cultural impacts on how the built environment was used. During periods of prosperity, most communities took little note of the impacts on the natural environment or the loss of early buildings in the name of progress. During periods of robust prosperity, a mindset emerged in the public that new was always better because it was an outward display of prosperity, facilitated by the increasing ease of replacing all manner of objects, including buildings. Throughout the last three centuries, time-honored traditional building materials and practices gave way to methods and materials that were cheaper to acquire or easier to install. These consumerist behaviors fostered today's widespread throwaway mentality. By the late twentieth century, this mindset became acutely prominent as consumerism reached an all-time high. As Gary Cross (2000: 3), professor of history at Pennsylvania State University, noted in *An All-Consuming Century*, "Consumerism had no interest in linking the present to the past and future." Therefore, new was predominantly viewed as better, and keeping something old implied a lack of ability to create or acquire something new. People (and communities) preferring to keep old things were portrayed as somehow lacking in ability, vision, or wherewithal to keep up with changing times.

As a result, the cumulative building design and construction practices of the late twentieth century led noted environmentalist Stewart Brand (1994: 2) to observe,

Almost no buildings adapt well. They're designed not to adapt; also budgeted and financed not to, constructed not to, administered not to, maintained not to, regulated and taxed not to. But all buildings (except monuments) adapt any-way, however poorly, because the usages in and around them are constantly changing.

Although early forms of building preservation occurred in the United States at the start of the nineteenth century (box 1.2), the overall effort was uneven across the country. In a nation that valued everything new, the notion of sav-ing something old was antithetical to popular beliefs. However, a few organi-zations championed the cause. Beyond the early efforts to establish national parks and monuments that led to the creation of the National Park Service in 1916, a number of statewide and regional organizations (e.g., Association for the Preservation of Virginia Antiquities, Association for the Preservation of New England Antiquities, and the Essex Institute) were formed to promote a greater understanding of preservation on a more local basis. Local historical societies also led efforts along these lines. However, two efforts emerged in the 1920s that brought preservation and respect for the past to the forefront in the public eye: the 1926 restoration of Colonial Williamsburg in Virginia and the 1929 creation of Greenfield Village in Dearborn, Michigan.

Colonial Williamsburg, backed by John D. Rockefeller, had the unprec-edented goal of restoring an entire colonial era village within an existing townscape that included not only removing the cultural overlay of buildings and additions constructed after the colonial era but also reconstructing the long-missing Capitol building. Greenfield Village, backed by industrialist Henry Ford, presented the opportunity to interpret buildings and building arts through the lens of mechanical trades and used buildings collected from around the United States and Europe to illustrate that connection.

Meanwhile, public efforts in the early 1930s to promote historic preserva-tion brought about the creation of the first two historic districts in the nation: the Old and Historic Charleston district in Charleston, South Carolina and the Vieux Carre district (i.e., the French Quarter) in New Orleans, Louisi-ana. In 1935, the US Congress enacted the Historic Sites Act, which, as his-torian Charles B. Hosmer Jr. noted in *With Heritage So Rich*, "was a great step forward in committing the Department of the Interior to a program that went beyond a mere caretaker role" (National Trust for Historic Preservation 1983: 10). This act established the authority for the National Park Service, as an operating unit within the Department of the Interior, to identify sites of

Box 1.2

US Historic Preservation Timeline

1816	Philadelphia purchases Independence Hall to protect it from demolition.
1850	New York purchases the Hasbrouck House and establishes the nation's first house museum.
1853	Ann Pamela Cunningham initiates efforts to save George Washington's Mount Vernon estate.
1872	Yellowstone is established as the nation's first national park.
1888	Association for the Preservation of Virginia Antiquities is formed.
1889	America's first National Monument designation is awarded to Casa Grande, near Coolidge, Arizona.
1890	Chickamauga Battlefield becomes the first National Military Park.
1906	Antiquities Act is passed to preserve prehistoric sites.
1909	Essex Institute opens America's first outdoor museum of historic buildings in Salem, Massachusetts.
1910	Society for the Preservation of New England Antiquities is incorporated.
1916	National Park Service is established and takes control of nine existing national monuments.
1926	Williamsburg restoration is funded by John D. Rockefeller.
1929	Greenfield Village, Henry Ford's collection of historic buildings and artifacts, opens to the public.
1931	Charleston establishes the first historic district ordinance in the United States.
1933	National Park Service is given responsibility for battlefields and other historic federal property.
	Historic American Buildings Survey is initiated.
1935	National Historic Sites Act is passed to identify national landmarks and acquire historic property.
1936	Louisiana creates commission to preserve the Vieux Carre in New Orleans.
1949	National Trust for Historic Preservation (NTHP) is chartered by Congress.
1966	National Historic Preservation Act is passed.
1967	State historic preservation officers and the first keeper of the National Register of Historic Places are appointed.
1968	Association for Preservation Technology International is formed.
1969	National Environmental Policy Act is passed.
	Historic American Engineering Record is established.
1970	First Earth Day is celebrated.
1971	Executive Order 11593 mandates federal preservation, restoration, and maintenance of cultural properties.

1972	Congress authorizes transfer of surplus historically significant properties to local public agencies.
1976	American Bicentennial strengthens interest in preservation.
	Tax Reform Act provides major tax incentives for historic preservation.
1977	National Trust's Main Street Project, forerunner of the National Main Street Center, is launched.
1978	New York City's preservation law is declared constitutional by the US Supreme Court.
1980	National Historic Preservation Act is amended.
1981	Economic Recovery Tax Act broadens tax credits for historic preservation.
1986	Tax Reform Act reduces opportunities for preservation tax credits.
1990	Charleston Principles are articulated.
1999	Save America's Treasures program is funded by Congress.
2000	Historic American Landscape Survey is established.
2008	NTHP launches its Sustainability Initiative.
	NTHP issues the Pocantico Proclamation.
2009	Preservation Green Lab is created.

Sources: Dwight (1993); National Park Service (2010c); Moe (2008); NTHP (2008, 2010a, 2010b).

national significance and accept them into the National Park Service holdings. Concurrently, Secretary of the Interior Harold Ickes sent J. Thomas Schneider to Europe to investigate European practices that could inform future preservation efforts in the United States (NTHP 1983: 10). The diverse European perspectives provide many insights on how to conduct historic preservation that continue to inform (and, some might say, confuse) how preservation is practiced in the United States today (box 1.3). With the rise of successful European efforts in reusing buildings as part of their sustainability strategies, these practices continue to demonstrate the important connection that preserving and reusing buildings can have in achieving sustainability.

In 1946, with the conclusion of World War II, preservation efforts to repair war-damaged Europe led the United Nations to form the United Nations Educational, Scientific and Cultural Organization (UNESCO). The growing credibility of UNESCO efforts worldwide played an important role in crafting what eventually became known as the Venice Charter in 1964, which in turn informed the National Historic Preservation Act (NHPA) of 1966 and

Box 1.3

A Fundamental Debate: Scrape versus Anti-Scrape

In eighteenth-century France, Eugene-Emmanuel Viollet-le-Duc advocated that "to restore an edifice means neither to maintain it, nor repair it, nor to rebuild it; it means to reestablish a finished state which in fact may never have existed at any given time" (Semes 2009: 117). Essentially, this implied removing any subsequent changes and crafting a restoration that was based on "critical analysis," which included a studied and scientific investigation as to what the design was intended to be. He was considered the leading expert in France, and his work forms the basis for what is now commonly called the "scrape" approach to preservation, where his "new work was scrupulously based on similar elements in buildings of the same region, date, proportions, and type," even when there was neither existing physical evidence nor documentation to support the new work (Semes 2009: 118).

Subsequently in England, John Ruskin and his follower William Morris led the debate over appropriate approaches to preserving and restoring buildings and advocated maintenance as the best form of preservation. Their perspectives foreshadowed the underlying principles of stewardship of the built environment, where greater respect must be paid to buildings that have stood the test of time through the use of high-quality materials and proper maintenance. They decried the approach to preservation wherein subsequent additions were removed in the name of restoration. Their position was that these accretions were part of the document of the history of the building and worthy of retention. In contrast to Viollet-le-Duc and the "scrape" approach, adherents to this "anti-scrape" approach held that the removal of subsequent additions was completely unnecessary (Stubbs 2009; Semes 2009; Stubbs and Makas 2011).

These two approaches to preservation contribute to a significant ongoing debate as to what constitutes appropriate preservation. The Venice Charter of 1964 essentially established the anti-scrape approach as the fundamental underlying premise of what appropriate practice should be.

the Secretary of the Interior Standards. Today UNESCO includes 193 member nations (including the United States) and has become the primary arbiter of what constitutes acceptable preservation (i.e., conservation) practices today (UNESCO 2011a). UNESCO has created a portfolio of World Heritage Sites that include both natural and cultural (human-made) resources that are deemed critically significant to understanding the heritage of the world. In the United States, these include such natural resources as the Yellowstone

National Park, Grand Canyon National Park, and Yosemite National Park and such cultural resources as the Statue of Liberty, Mesa Verde National Park, and Independence Hall (UNESCO 2011b).

In the 1940s, the National Park Service found that it could not complete "any survey work, major restoration or acquisition of historic properties except where prewar appropriations were still available" (NTHP 1983: 10). As a result, the Department of the Interior recognized the need for an organization to promote preservation, resulting in Congress's chartering of the NTHP in 1949. Modeled after the British National Trust, the NTHP established programs in education, publications, property management, and field services.

Throughout the 1950s, the NTHP's efforts at promoting its cause were quite successful; as Hosmer again noted, "a new interest in historic preservation began to sweep across the nation" (NTHP 1983: 10). In numerous instances, the loss of a beloved historic building such as the 1963 demolition of Penn Station in New York City led to the formation of local preservation advocacy groups. The NTHP and these local-based preservation-oriented groups cultivated support for preservation that secured passage of the NHPA of 1966, which regulates activities involving historic resources of national interest. These activities are discussed in detail in chapter 2. Public awareness of the importance of understanding history through the retention of and respect for significant buildings, structures, and sites had finally gained national attention. Initially, the strategy to save buildings occurred almost entirely on an emotional level wherein proponents for saving a particular building tried to gain support by appealing to people's sense of history, nostalgia, or emotional attachment. In turn, local municipalities began creating various ordinances protecting historic resources. Developers wanting to demolish or make alterations that would substantially compromise the historic integrity of a building challenged these laws. A prime example was the landmark 1978 case of *Penn Central Transportation Company v. City of New York*, in which the plaintiff disputed the defendant's authority to regulate the development of a designated historic property. Penn Central wanted to construct a fifty-five-story addition over the Grand Central Station building, which was a designated local landmark. The City of New York denied the permit. The US Supreme Court ultimately decided in favor of the City of New York, creating the precedent that proved "the legitimacy of historic preservation review ordinances by recognizing that preserving historic resources is a permissible governmental goal and the city's preservation ordinance was an appropriate means for accomplishing that goal" (Tyler, Ligibel, and Tyler 2009: 123–126).

As the preservation movement matured throughout the late twentieth century, it looked beyond nostalgia to a sustainable future; thus, preserving and reusing buildings as a sustainability strategy has gained greater attention over the past several decades. Nurturing this nascent acceptance is at the core of the stewardship of the built environment philosophy.

Environmental Contributions of Preservation and Reuse

In addition to the significant social contributions of preserving and reusing buildings, there are long-reaching environmental benefits as well. The primary environmental contributions of preservation and reuse regarding the physical environment are to relieve growth pressures at the suburban periphery and thereby protect open lands, reduce depletion of natural resources (e.g., nonrenewable energy, raw materials), curtail the flow of building demolition materials into landfills, improve atmospheric quality by reducing reliance on automobiles, and revitalize existing neighborhoods and commercial districts in a manner that directly parallels many of the smart growth principles currently being promoted nationwide.

Ecological Approach to Viewing the Environment

A key to understanding how to foster sustainability is to view the environment as a closed-loop ecological system composed of the natural environment and the built environment in which *each generates waste products that provide symbiotic benefits to the other.* One example is the oxygen–carbon dioxide exchange in which plants consume carbon dioxide and produce oxygen. Conversely, inhabitants, transportation, conventional power production, and manufacturing systems consume oxygen and produce carbon dioxide (and other chemical compounds). When the exchanges are in balance, a sustainable environment exists in which *each component has the capacity to carry loads imposed by the other.*

In the nonsustainable view of the world, the natural environment seemingly had infinite capacity to absorb the wastes generated by people (fig. 1.6). This

Figure 1.6. In many early settlement periods, the natural environment was seen as vast and something that needed to be tamed. This was the predominant perception during the settlement of North America.

view arose when the human population was small compared with the natural environment around it. In American society, this perception often led to a frontier mentality, which mistakenly assumes there will always be something more or better elsewhere after wastefulness has depleted the social, environmental, or economic resources of the current place. As the human population continues to grow beyond 7 billion, however, this perspective has proven to be flawed: Nature no longer has endless capacity to absorb those wastes as our built environments have become contiguous, dense concentrations of people and buildings instead of the loosely dispersed range of settlements common in preindustrial landscapes.

The original mutually symbiotic relationship between the built and natural environments changes as the built environment increasingly encroaches on and diminishes the overall quality of the local natural environment. The rise of sprawl through unregulated new development threatens the open space and farmland that otherwise contribute to sustainable ecological balance. Intensified land use creates excessive waste products that initially stress the environment locally, then regionally, and ultimately globally. One example is the increased reliance on automobiles for transportation to, from, and within the urban core and its suburbs. As vehicle miles traveled increase, the resulting exhaust emissions deteriorate air quality. Originally most notable in Los Angeles, California, this emission-based decline is now present in cities nationwide and around the world. As these increased waste pressures from a sprawling built environment approach or exceed the capacity of the natural environment, both the built and natural environment decline. When coupled with other industrial emissions, this decline becomes a regional problem as the pollution fouls the airshed with greenhouse gases that create respiratory problems, acidification of rain, soils, and groundwater, and a poorer quality of life.

This decline accelerates when only one or two SEE components are considered. The lack of concurrent consideration may be detrimental to the excluded components. For instance, constructing an electrical generation plant may raise living standards socially, provide jobs for utility workers, and increase profitability for the power company, but unless its negative environmental impacts (e.g., creating air pollution, destroying habitats, generating radioactive waste, and increasing suburban sprawl) are minimized, the project would not be considered sustainable design.

The Rise of Sprawl

How did Americans transform a vast natural environment into the complex megalopolis that exists today? To better understand this transformation, a brief orientation on historical land use patterns is needed. Throughout history, little heed was given to the effects of industrialization on the built and natural environments, especially where natural resources were exploited for profit. This extraction and depletion philosophy has predominantly shaped land use in the United States. Once existing resources ran out, other sources for natural resources were sought out, and this cycle repeated.

In a similar manner, population migration became the prevalent practice for those seeking a better life financially, politically, or spiritually. As the industrial revolution occurred, the population in cities and towns grew more concentrated and living conditions declined. As a reaction, westward expansion accelerated as people sought a better life elsewhere. Boom towns emerged rapidly when a significant natural resource was discovered or a significant manufacturing venture was established locally. However, as the available natural resources or the economic demand for a product declined, the ensuing bust period often forced people to move away. This is certainly evident in the numerous abandoned business operations left behind (fig. 1.7).

Transportation plays an important role not only in the productivity and profitability of cities, states, and regions but also in how people move from place to place. Before mechanically driven vehicles were invented, transportation by human- or animal-powered means kept cities and communities compact. Ships and trains expanded the range of travel throughout the nineteenth century, but the introduction of fossil fuel–based automobiles at the turn of the twentieth century dramatically expanded the range of transportation available to the common person. The start of the interstate highway system in 1956 further changed the built environment by enabling even faster transit to suburban locations. Cheap land became the destination for home builders and real estate developers and, subsequently, new home buyers and businesses. Eventually the frontier mentality and the desire to make financial gains prompted investors to build further into the suburbs. Conversely, the working- and middle-class citizenry, enticed once again by the opportunity for a better life, began moving to the suburbs.

Figure 1.7. As resources were depleted or markets shifted, operations were closed. This seriously hurt local boom towns and often left contaminated sites.

In the late twentieth century, while many metropolitan areas increased in population overall, the city core population shrank as people moved to the interstate-based suburbs. Today, these cities and their growing suburbs constitute a burgeoning megalopolis, especially east of the Mississippi River and along the west coast. The increased reliance on automobiles and commuting between downtown offices and increasingly distant suburbs threatens long- and short-term human health through air pollution and the production of greenhouse gases. This nonsustainability is further compounded when the costs of expanding and maintaining infrastructure are included. Though particularly evident in communities with greater automobile dependency (e.g., Atlanta and Los Angeles), an alternative paradigm is more commonly found in Europe, where cities are more compact and more likely to accommodate non-motorized private transportation (e.g., bicycles or walking) or provide mass transit systems.

The frontier mentality and growth forces that fueled sprawl in the late twentieth century also fostered the idea that new is always better. In expanding the suburban periphery, not only did this preclude reusing existing buildings in the inner city and first-tier early suburbs, it also ignored the numerous sustainable advantages that urbanism engenders. Missing were the walkable communities, the sense of place, and the cultural diversity that were replaced by an automobile-dependent and socioculturally homogenous population.

Land use trends at the turn of the twenty-first century included new urbanism, transit-oriented design, walkable communities, and smart growth. Although each draws from urban concepts common in preindustrial urban centers (e.g., intermingled uses, short walking distances, diverse populations), developers built many of the more notable projects in the suburbs (e.g., Celebration, Florida). Few incorporated public transit, and the result was increased sprawl, vehicle miles traveled, utility and infrastructure costs, air pollution, and separation of population and land uses. Meanwhile, urban centers continued to decline.

With a seemingly insatiable appetite for open land and focus on new construction, development continues in the suburban periphery. Currently in the United States, 1 million acres of agricultural land is converted to use for buildings annually (Carroon 2010: 8) with much of that conversion occurring for housing (fig. 1.8). This process clearly reveals the American attitude that farmland and undeveloped land are temporary uses and is a distinct contrast

Figure 1.8. The Euclidean zoning system used in the United States has fostered sprawl in areas surrounding major urban centers and has led to an increased reliance on automobiles for transportation and the reduction of local agricultural production.

to the European attitude about rural land conservation. As Timothy Beatley, professor of sustainable communities at the University of Virginia, describes in *Green Urbanism*, "European rural and agricultural land uses are not seen as transient activities but as important societal uses," and he further states, "Rural land, especially agricultural land, is preciously guarded" (Beatley 2000: 58). In the United States, as population centers grow, undeveloped land in the urban core becomes scarce. When coupled with easy access to interstate freeways, the need to expand and accommodate a growing population fosters sprawl and growth pressures on open lands within and beyond the suburbs.

Emergence of a Sustainability Ethos

The language of sustainability has evolved from numerous sources, many of which conceive it as a form of stewardship and trusteeship. As political philosopher Michael J. Sandel of Harvard University explains (Friedman 2009: 237),

[Stewardship] involves responsibility for the natural world. It is born of wonder and awe of the diversity of life and the majesty of nature. Trusteeship involves responsibility for future generations, for those who will inhabit this place after our time.

This is the primary tenet of stewardship of the built environment. The decision process directly looks at how changes to the built environment affect the overall natural environment and subsequently how those effects can be enhanced or mitigated through judicious design and construction choices and practices so that future generations can benefit from them.

Although a number of countries worldwide recognize the importance of creating a sustainable relationship between the built and the natural environments, this recognition had not been fully valued in the United States even as late as the turn of the twenty-first century. Despite this obstacle and long before many people recognized the far-reaching implications of unchecked sprawl, environmental activists have been active throughout the development of the United States and included such notables as Henry David Thoreau, Ralph Waldo Emerson, John Muir, John Wesley Powell, Theodore Roosevelt, Aldo Leopold, Ansel Adams, Stephen Mather, Horace Albright, Gifford Pinchot, and Wallace Stegner, whose work was the foundation of the modern environmental movement. These thinkers espoused an approach to the relationship between humans and the natural environment that is more closely aligned with the preservation movement than many people might think.

The publication of such groundbreaking works as *Silent Spring* by Rachel Carson and *The Death and Life of Great American Cities* by Jane Jacobs spurred the actions of a number of environmental groups in the 1960s. Unfortunately, many of their concerns were dismissed by the established network of industrial manufacturers who controlled the political and social agendas through their ability to present themselves as the necessary impetus for continued progress. In addition to organizations such as the Sierra Club and the National Audubon Society, the NTHP took a leadership role in conservation through programs that promoted the retention of historically significant buildings, neighborhoods, and sites. Fortunately, as a result of the emerging political activism of these groups, this period saw the enactment of the NHPA of 1966 and, just 3 years later, the National Environmental Policy Act (NEPA) of 1969, which laid the groundwork for future progress by making the federal government accountable for how government funding and policy affect the built environment and natural environments (Dwight 1993: 120). Subsequent revisions to these laws and the enactment of other laws began to bring industries into conformance with national environmental goals.

The NHPA and NEPA created or enhanced several federal agencies and programs to provide an interface between the government and the public. From a preservation perspective, two of the three most prominent, the State Historic Preservation Offices (SHPO) program and the National Register of Historic Places (NRHP), began in 1967 as the federal agencies responsible for identifying historic resources (e.g., districts, sites, buildings, structures, and objects). The SHPO program created an office in each state to act as the federal information clearinghouse on policy and technical advice at the state level. In addition to preservation education and advocacy functions, the SHPO is the state administrator and coordinator for nominations to the NRHP and applications for federal and state tax incentive programs through the National Park Service.

The NRHP designates which resources have historic significance at the national, state, and local levels. Established in reaction to such federally backed programs as urban renewal and interstate highway construction, NRHP determines whether these resources can be included or are eligible for inclusion on the NRHP. Designation on the NRHP is intended primarily to protect these historic resources from adverse effects of projects funded with federal money. This includes federal funding for highway construction, low-income housing, and a variety of federal tax credits.

The third most prominent agency has been the Environmental Protection Agency (EPA), formed in 1970 in part to review environmental impact statements that included provisions for delineating the impact of a project on both natural and historic cultural resources. The NEPA of 1969 mandates that the EPA "preserve important historic, cultural, and natural aspects of our national heritage" (Advisory Council on Historic Preservation 2010).

Since these laws were passed, the growing recognition of historic preservation and adaptive use as a viable sustainability strategy in the early twenty-first century has increased its popularity nationwide. Post-9/11 attitudes about patriotism and heritage coupled with an economic recession have created an environment where people seek to reconnect with their national roots, celebrate the uniqueness of their communities, and reconsider the consumerist attitudes of the recent past. Although the significance of these perceptions has long been recognized in preservation and environmental conservation circles, this awareness is new to many Americans. Attitudes about consumerism are changing, and the appreciation for just how a community or region contributes to a sense of national heritage and community identity is growing. The growing green awareness has prompted a second look at what it means to respect, retain, and fully appreciate what the connections to the past and future have to offer while still meeting the demands of contemporary society.

As leaders began to recognize the need for a greater awareness of sustainability, policy makers began focusing on how to promote sustainable practices. Such legislation as the Environmental Policy Act (EPACT) of 1992 (updated and broadened in 2005 and 2010) defined numerous energy and water conservation policies and the discontinuation of production of a wide variety of inefficient and outdated lighting and electrical products (US Department of Energy 2010b) that affected energy consumption and sustainability in both new and existing buildings. Unfortunately, a potentially significant drawback of many of these policies, programs, standards, codes, and initiatives is that they are geared primarily toward new construction and overlook or ignore the mechanisms needed to apply them to existing buildings. Some initial attempts were made to mitigate their effects through the development of the Uniform Code for Building Conservation and its successor International Existing Building Code, which incorporate sensitivity to the disruption of historically significant and character-defining building materials and construction systems. These codes present alternative ways to interpret the code goals to enable retention of these materials and systems, but communities have not adopted them as widely as other new construction–oriented codes.

Additionally, a growing number of states (e.g., California, New Jersey, Maryland, and New York) have initiated what are now known as *smart codes*, which allow interpretation of code objectives to aid in retention of character-defining features in existing and historic buildings. Similarly, the specific issues of fire, safety, and accessibility (fig. 1.9) have prompted development of separate codes or provisions in local codes for direct implementation in existing and historic buildings.

For historic buildings that were built before the adoption of modern seismic codes, changes to a higher level of use may trigger the requirement for a seismic upgrade. For most buildings this means upgrading the structural systems to withstand the loads created during an earthquake. In many cases, this

Figure 1.9. The Americans with Disabilities Act mandates accessibility upgrades to public buildings. One solution has been to redefine the main entrance as adjoining the parking lot (commonly at the rear of the building), where access for the disabled can be achieved more readily without compromising the historic features of the traditional front entrance. Shown here is the Washington County Courthouse in St. George, Utah.

means installing additional bracing and stiffening the walls and floors, which can have significant effects on the appearance and performance of the building as structural bracing is inserted into occupied spaces. Seismic activity is particularly problematic for unreinforced masonry buildings, where the joints between the stone, block, or brick offer little resistance to failure during an earthquake. The cost of the seismic upgrade is significant and may be prohibitive if funding is not available. This expense is eligible for historic tax credits that would then trigger a review to determine compliance with the Secretary of the Interior's Standards.

Economic Contributions of Preservation and Reuse

The primary contributions that preserving and reusing buildings can make to economic sustainability are evident in the enhanced social, environmental, and economic vitality of the communities in which stewardship of the built environment has been practiced. We have already noted the social and environmental aspects, but the economic aspects are what drive most decision-making processes in the contemporary built environment. Recognition of the benefits of reusing existing and historic buildings emerged in the late 1960s, and by the mid-1970s federal, state, and local governments implemented a number of economic incentives (e.g., tax credits, grants, and special loan programs) that continue to this day. Although changes in the tax laws and government policies have caused fluctuations in available funding, the end result has been a growing positive effect on the retention of buildings and the resulting measurable enhancement of property values, economic activity, income tax generation, and job creation.

Specifically, the period just before the American bicentennial saw the successful completion of a number of significant adaptive reuse projects across the country. Coupled with favorable tax laws and incentives, the period from 1976 to 1986 saw a significant increase in the interest and intensity of historic preservation and adaptive reuse as a way to retain important historic fabric and cultural contexts while providing an attractive economic return on investment. Subsequent changes in the tax laws in 1986 redefined how investors could benefit financially from any investment property. Although this tax revision made a fundamental change in the way investors could fund the reuse and preservation of existing buildings, this decade of investment reenergized the preservation community as it demonstrated the economic and social benefits of preservation to the larger public. The period also produced a revitalization of moribund traditional building craft trades and saw the emergence of products and practices specifically geared toward the reuse and rehabilitation of existing buildings. More important, it created new job opportunities that were tied to the local community and could not be exported overseas.

As tax incentives and other funding opportunities grew and traditional building skills and products became more readily available, both real estate developers and preservationists demonstrated how reusing or rehabilitating existing buildings made economic sense (fig. 1.10). The success of a growing number of projects that reused and respected historic buildings was the first step in broadening the recognition of how preservation and reuse is a viable community development tool for economic sustainability. Building preservation and reuse has increasingly been acknowledged as a way to reinvest in a community and respect the cultural and social aspects of that community.

Figure 1.10. Trolley Square in Salt Lake City, Utah, converted to a shopping center in 1972, was an early demonstration that preservation could revitalize buildings and districts.

When it came to extending these ideas to the community scale, the NTHP recognized that most small communities lacked the expertise to organize the economic restructuring of their central business districts to accommodate preserving and reusing buildings effectively. Therefore, the NTHP launched the National Main Street Project, forerunner of its National Main Street Center (NMSC) program, in 1980 to provide educational and technical assistance. In addition, many states and preservation advocacy groups introduced incentives such as state tax credits, low-interest loans, and grant programs.

Preservation and Reuse as an Economic Engine

Several metrics define the economic impact and benefits of economic development programs. These include job creation, community income, retail sales, and tax revenue. For preservation and reuse programs, these metrics are compelling, especially when compared with either new construction or the primary industries associated with a particular state or region. Every million dollars spent on rehabilitation creates 5–9 more local construction jobs, creates 4.7

additional jobs in the community, generates $107,000 more community income, and generates $34,000 more in retail sales than the same amount spent on new construction (National Conference of State Historic Preservation Officers 2010) and typically can create more jobs than a million dollars spent on an individual state's primary industry (e.g., 22 more jobs than cutting timber in Oregon) (Rypkema 2005: 11). In addition, the skilled labor–intensive jobs created by rehabilitation can be sustained indefinitely even if only 2–3 percent of the local building stock is rehabilitated annually (Mize 2009).

Furthermore, Main Street revitalization programs in more than 1,700 communities nationwide have used $23 billion in public and private reinvestment funds that have created 310,000 net new jobs, or the equivalent cost of $2,500 per job generated (Rypkema 2008). Along these lines, the Save America's Treasures grant program has created 16,012 new jobs at a cost of $13,780 per job (Rypkema 2010). When compared with the recent American Recovery and Reinvestment Act, which created only four new jobs per million dollars spent (i.e., $250,000 per job), this is a tremendous level of achievement. The income generated by these jobs contributes to tax revenues but also is spent within the community and state. The National Main Street Center reported in 2010 that each dollar spent on operating a local Main Street program generated $40.35 in return to the community (NMSC 2010c).

From a regulatory perspective, state and federal governments have enacted a variety of programs and incentives that promote the preservation and reuse of buildings. A variety of grant and loan programs that vary by state are available for planning and rehabilitation projects that preserve and reuse buildings. In addition to a Historic Tax Credit (HTC) that provides a 20 percent tax credit or a 10 percent tax credit (depending on project specifications) to cover qualified rehabilitation expenses, the federal government provides two tax credits— low-income housing tax credits and new market tax credits—that provide tax relief for rehabilitating existing buildings (and for new construction). These programs can each be coupled with the HTC when a historic building is being rehabilitated or applied separately when an existing building is to be reused. The HTC has become more popular as a financing strategy as its familiarity increases. Tax credit syndication groups have further accelerated the desirability of these credits as syndicators purchase the credits up front (and recoup them in future tax years), and the project owners can use this money for an enhanced equity position or other uses that increase the marketability of the project. The actual economic impact and metrics of the HTC program are discussed in further detail in chapter 4. Other support for the importance of preserving and reusing buildings is indicated by the government's revised tax codes, which remove earlier advantages that new construction had held over reusing buildings.

At the local level, although many believe that historic designation of a property freezes or even reduces a property's value, properties in designated historic districts and neighborhoods invariably *appreciate at a faster rate than similar buildings outside those districts*. Although there are numerous case studies on this phenomenon, Donovan Rypkema (2002a: 6) reports in *Cultural Resource Management* that

> Using a variety of methodologies, conducted by a number of independent researchers, this analysis has been undertaken in New Jersey, Texas, Indiana, Georgia, Colorado, Maryland, North and South Carolina, Kentucky, Virginia, and elsewhere. The results of these studies are remarkably consistent: property values in local historic districts appreciate significantly faster than the market as a whole in the vast majority of cases and appreciate at rates equivalent to the market in the worst case. Simply put—local historic districts enhance property values.

Accordingly, increased property values translate into increased property tax revenues for the local community.

One further testament to the sustainable economic contribution of preserving and reusing buildings is the emergence of what is now called the cultural heritage tourist. These tourists specifically "travel to experience the arts or history of a location or travel to immerse oneself in the language, society, or culture of a region" (Travel Industry Dictionary.com 2011), which includes architecture and cultural landscapes. The American bicentennial revived interest in cultural heritage and enhanced interest in places of historical importance. This resulting cultural heritage tourism trend continues to this day and, in a post-9/11 world, has benefited from the growing popularity of "staycations" and attention to local cultures, foods, and the traditions that inform them. Studies show that heritage tourists stay longer and spend more money per capita than other types of tourists.

Land Use from an Economic-Based Decision Process

Economic sustainability directly creates opportunities for the preservation and reuse of buildings. In economically expanding times, money is available to invest in building construction activities, in both new construction and rehabilitation. Paradoxically, this presents both an opportunity and a dilemma for preserving and reusing buildings wherein money can be used to promote rehabilitation directly or fund building replacement or new construction. Given the goals of stewardship of the built environment, it is hoped that the former can gain more popularity. Conversely, in economically contracting times, little funding exists for either new or reuse construction activities. Coupled with declining population, this can cause substantial loss of the built environment as community leaders attempt to "right size" their cities and find new economic activities to reestablish economic stability. Preservation and reuse promotes many of the same aspects of good urban design that people now define as smart growth and can provide substantial insights into how to assist communities in this process.

The migrations of businesses and workers were an early characteristic of settlement and land use patterns across the United States that were driven largely by economic processes that persist to this day. These processes work bilaterally where owners seek to maximize profit and workers seek to increase their standard of living. Since the mid-twentieth century, local-scale development has continued to expand into spaces previously used for agriculture and recreation. As noted earlier, highways and public utility infrastructures have expanded to accommodate further sprawl. This has initiated a spiral of increasing costs of living, increasing costs for new infrastructure, increasing health problems, and emerging political and social unrest. Furthermore, as growth continues without the inclusion of public mass transit, water and air are increasingly fouled and natural resources are depleted.

Although undeveloped suburban land initially is cheaper than that available in the urban core, subsequent increases in social and environmental costs have been identified as nonsustainable and come with long-term economically unsustainable consequences in terms of health care and social justice. Moreover, because of a lack of local availability or economic competition from elsewhere, raw materials for construction, manufactured goods, and agricultural products are increasingly imported from greater distances.

Business decisions based solely on economic considerations foster the relocation of various industries and agricultural market sources to areas where labor costs and oversight regulations are less burdensome. Although it is now being practiced on a global scale, the results of this practice on a domestic scale are evident in North America, where manufacturing industries (e.g., automobiles, textiles, and shoes) relocated operations from the northern industrialized (and unionized) locations to the south and west and, eventually, overseas to emerging industrial nations where labor costs were lower.

This migration trend at the local and regional scale has left a significant number of built resources available for retrofit and reuse through economic repurposing as communities seek to increase their economic vitality and become more sustainable. The automotive manufacturing industry is a good contemporary example of this migratory trend. Opportunities for good-paying jobs brought workers from rural locations to the upper Midwest in the early to mid-twentieth century. Subsequently, competition from foreign manufacturers caused a significant reduction in the profitability of automobile-related industries. With growing union strength, companies sought to close manufacturing facilities in areas where the resulting labor costs were high and open new ones where labor costs were low. This fostered growth in the non-unionized "right-to-work" states. Increased unemployment caused workers to follow the work opportunities and fostered migration from the Rust Belt to the Sun Belt. These economic shifts and migrations leave a significantly underused built environment that is ripe for demolition or other endeavors that have many preservation and reuse implications.

Sustainable Stewardship

Although innumerable buildings are renovated and remodeled each year, the preservation and reuse movement became a catalyst in numerous projects ranging from the rehabilitation of a single building (which has frequently led to the rehabilitation of buildings in its surrounding neighborhood) to the broader revitalization of central business districts. The economic incentives coupled with the social and environmental agendas of a growing number of stewardship advocates have broadened the exposure and demonstrated the appeal of preserving and reusing buildings (historic or otherwise). This observation has been borne out by the many successful examples of revitalization efforts that had embraced preservation and reuse across the country by the turn of the twenty-first century (fig. 1.11). Although preservation tax credits are available only for properties on or eligible for the National Register of Historic Places, there are parallels in the application of these stewardship principles to existing nonhistoric buildings, which can promote sustainability goals more quickly than relying on new construction alone.

The NTHP has emerged as an acknowledged leader in preservation advocacy and has continued to raise awareness of the environmental benefits of retaining buildings through preservation and reuse by establishing its *Sustainability Initiative*. In 2008, the NTHP convened a symposium at the Pocantico Center in Tarrytown, New York to explore approaches to preservation and sustainability in the twenty-first century. The Pocantico Proclamation that materialized from that symposium is guided by the principles that resonate throughout this book: reuse, reinvest, retrofit, and respect (NTHP 2008). Richard Moe, then president of the NTHP, described these as the four core tenets of what he calls sustainable stewardship:

Reuse buildings: A sound older building that is abandoned or underused is a wasted asset. Putting existing buildings to good use reduces demolition and construction waste, lessens the demand for energy and other resources for new building materials, and conserves the energy originally expended to create these structures.

Reinvest in older and historic neighborhoods. . . . While sprawl devours our landscape, neighborhoods in the inner city and the inner ring of suburbs are vastly underused. Revitalization of existing neighborhoods promotes efficient land-use patterns and focuses public and private reinvestments in areas where infrastructure is already in place, already paid for. Furthermore, older neighborhoods are typically compact, centrally-located, walkable, and mass-transit accessible—characteristics that are promoted by advocates of smart growth and the "new urbanism."

Retrofit older and historic buildings to achieve energy efficiency. . . . Many older buildings are remarkably energy-efficient. . . . Nevertheless, many older buildings are badly in need of energy-efficiency upgrades—and there are plenty of techniques and products on the market that make these upgrades much less challenging than they once were.

Figure 1.11. Preservation has evolved and matured by moving from iconic house museums such as the Paul Revere House (shown in fig. 1.5) to revitalizing cities both large and small with projects such as Faneuil Hall Marketplace in Boston, Massachusetts.

Respect historic integrity: An increasing number of sensitive and successful rehab projects demonstrate that historic buildings can go green without losing the distinctive character that makes them significant and appealing. Architects, developers and property owners no longer have to choose between getting the energy-efficiency they want or keeping the character they love; they can have both. (Moe 2008)

In conclusion, the direction we must take can best be summed up in the words of Carl Elefante: "We cannot build our way to sustainability; we must conserve our way to it" (Kienle 2008).

From this overview, you can begin to understand why preservation and reuse has not gained a larger segment of activity in the construction industry despite evidence that it is a profitable (and, in contemporary terms, sustainable) enterprise. Beyond the primary focus on new construction, both misperceptions about the social necessity of preserving and reusing buildings and the current approach of treating undeveloped lands as the frontier that needs to be civilized have contributed to the continued unsustainable expansion into open lands at the suburban periphery. However, as evidence mounts on the long-term implications of preserving and reusing buildings, more people are becoming aware of its long-term value. So instead of questioning why we should preserve buildings, they are seeking strategies and insights that tell them how to do so. In the chapters that follow, we will look at the factors that determine how and why preserving and reusing buildings is at the heart of appropriate stewardship of the built environment and the means to get there.

CHAPTER TWO
Social Factors

Preserving and reusing buildings can be a significant part of transforming urban environments into sustainable cities. Social trends in the early twenty-first century indicate a growing interest in living in urban areas that provide a good quality of life, short work commute, walkability, local culture and entertainment opportunities, and a sense of place. The adoption of stewardship principles will require efforts from a broad spectrum of people who understand the social benefits and opportunities that preservation and reuse can provide. From professional practitioners in design, construction, and planning to community leaders, property owners, and private citizens, the key to adopting a stewardship approach will be attaining the skills and insights needed to create a more sustainable environment.

The social factors affecting the continued growth and acceptance of preserving and reusing buildings are broad and pervasive and need to be better recognized and understood. This chapter examines the social benefits of revitalizing the built and natural environment and explores the tools, processes, and sociopolitical framework of contemporary preservation and reuse practices that in turn can shape twenty-first-century policies and perceptions. It concludes with a look at emerging initiatives and trends.

Seeking Urbanism: Social Implications for Preservation and Reuse

The preservation and reuse opportunities of the late twentieth and early twenty-first centuries emerged in a built environment that was devastated by the urban renewal and highway construction programs that began in the 1940s. The Housing Act of 1949 authorized funds to clear slums and promote urban redevelopment that emphasized new construction (US Department of Housing and Urban Development [HUD] 2010b). The Highway Act of 1956 provided funding to extend the interstate highway system into inner cities. As a result, a substantial portion of inner-city neighborhoods were demolished. The urban renewal zones did not specifically identify buildings to be saved, and subsequently, the view emerged that a completely cleared site would best facilitate redevelopment and the economic stimulation that urban renewal implied. In addition to blighted buildings, architecturally sound buildings were removed. As cultural geographers Jakle and Wilson note in *Derelict Landscapes* (1992: 133),

> Total clearance was not necessary to the renewal of cities, but it fit the tenor of the times. A generation frustrated by the economic Great Depression, but bolstered by the triumphs of World War II, little appreciated its inheritance from the past. Modernism had come to dominate architectural design. New buildings stripped of all past symbolism, floated as isolated objects, contrasting boldly with their surroundings.

In this early period of urban revitalization, the removal of complete neighborhoods caused significant displacement of their inhabitants. As community-less tenants looked for new places to live, they joined others displaced from similar project zones, compounding the loss of community identity. In 1960, Vance Packard, journalist, social critic, and author of *The Waste Makers*, observed,

> The challenge of tackling urban blight in the United States does not necessarily mean tearing down miles of buildings and replacing them with thirty-story concrete slabs. . . . Inhabitants would be happier if they simply have their old neighborhood homes and streets spruced up with some pleasant open spaces added. (Jakle and Wilson 1992: 134)

This statement presciently describes the approach used in many historic districts in the late twentieth century.

The Housing Act of 1949, amended in 1954 and 1956, provides funding for rehabilitation and conservation of deteriorating areas. This gradual shift from new construction to conservation had a major impact on the formation of today's housing policies, in which options for rehabilitation are encouraged and demolition is no longer the only course of action. This trend continued into the 1960s and 1970s. In 1965, the Housing and Urban Development Act established the Department of Housing and Urban Development (HUD) as a cabinet-level agency (HUD 2010d). The Housing and Community Development Act of 1974 established the Community Development Block Grant program to further encourage redeveloping neighborhoods and properties (HUD 2010b).

Even without considering the loss of historic fabric, many urban renewal programs were viewed as less than successful. A common realization in the aftermath of urban renewal was that the failure of the anticipated redevelopment often left land vacant for years, or when some form of redevelopment was completed, it created poorly designed areas that were little better than what they replaced (Porter 2002: 118). In many cities, renewal zones enabled the demolition of a viable urban context and replaced it with an amalgamation of parking lots and low-intensity uses akin to suburban strip malls or with sterile urban centers that were largely deserted at the end of the work day.

In some areas, the neighborhoods and commercial districts adjoining these zones continued to decline as financing systems and processes favored the suburbs. Through the 1940–1970 period of suburban flight, disinvestment was compounded by economic downturns in various cities. Property values declined, and existing owner-occupied buildings were often converted to absentee rentals. Many of the people remaining in the inner city and first-tier suburban neighborhoods could not afford to move, could not find buyers with financing to whom they could sell their property, had no desire to give up their neighborhood connections, or felt powerless to act. Limitations on financing, lack of demand for inner-city housing, and lack of incentives prevented redevelopment. Many properties declined or were abandoned outright.

Changing priorities through the 1970s and 1980s from demolition to rehabilitation began to make their mark with federal funding that carried down to local governments. With these changes in how the built environment was valued came a renewed interest in urban living. The city of Baltimore sponsored an urban homesteading program in 1973 in which those interested in city living could purchase a house for $1 (foreclosed or held by the city for unpaid taxes). The restriction was that the house had to be brought up to code within 6 months, and the owner had to live there for at least 18 months (DeCourcy Hinds 1986: 2). This program was replicated in other cities such as Philadelphia, Pennsylvania and Wilmington, Delaware.

Since the post–World War II period urban pioneers, attracted to lower property costs and good locations, have purchased declining properties and rehabbed them. This trend, led by artists and others seeking less expensive places to live and people wanting to reduce or eliminate commuting who initiated low-level private revitalization efforts in urban neighborhoods, has led to spectacular results. The most notable among these are South of Houston Street (Soho) and Triangle Below Canal (Tribeca) in New York City. Yet this practice extends nationwide with examples such as the Old Port in Portland, Maine and, more recently, the Pearl District in Portland, Oregon (fig. 2.1). Although too many exist to list here, neighborhoods and business districts throughout the country have experienced the social, environmental, and economic benefits of this phenomenon.

Buoyed by the successes of the do-it-yourself trend and coupled with increasing number of public–private partnerships that have generated successful adaptive use projects throughout the country, a renewed interest in city living emerged. However, success of these projects has led to problems as they have driven up property values, increased rents, and attracted even larger redevelopment projects that threaten to price out current inhabitants. As often happens, these successes also induce expansion of these projects into surrounding neighborhoods, which may further displace longtime residents.

Without government protection, older neighborhoods are vulnerable to market forces, such as property owners building "monster homes" (fig. 2.2) after demolishing the original buildings. In this form of gentrification, the property owner is attracted to amenities of the local neighborhood (e.g., cultural

Figure 2.1. The Old Port in Portland, Maine (left) and the Pearl District in Portland, Oregon (right). Rehabilitation of warehouse districts has become a coast-to-coast phenomenon.

Figure 2.2. "Monster homes" typically are built in neighborhoods without design review oversight and often without regard to neighbors' privacy and access to views and sunlight. Although they meet zoning ordinances and building codes, their scale and massing do not fit in with the adjoining buildings.

events, social and aesthetic diversity, proximity to work, alternative transportation options, social institutions, and medical facilities) but deems the housing stock too small. In 1950, the average house size was 983 square feet. By 2004, this average had grown to 2,349 square feet (Solomon 2009). Reports of single-family homes reaching several thousand square feet were becoming increasingly common until the real estate market declines of the past several years. This consumerist desire to have several thousand square feet of living space often conflicts with the typical size of a house built 50 or more years ago. Older neighborhoods are therefore at risk for demolitions and a variety of alterations that lead to the creation of monster homes, also known as blowouts, popups, McMansions, starter castles, and garage mahals.

As noted in the National Trust for Historic Preservation (NTHP) information bulletin *Protecting America's Historic Neighborhoods: Taming the Teardown Trend*, the desire for a garage mahal is "another example of how we sometimes carelessly throw away our valuable heritage in the name of progress and change." The impact on existing neighborhoods is twofold: The architectural heritage is eroded (and consigned to a landfill), and the massive structures do not fit well into historic neighborhoods and "threaten the very qualities that make these neighborhoods attractive and desirable" (Fine and Lindberg 2002: 2).

Recent trends indicate that new houses are getting smaller, which may lessen the disruption caused by this phenomenon. Arthur C. Nelson, director of the Metropolitan Research Center at the University of Utah, has published research indicating that by 2030, households with children will drop to 27 percent (down from 33 percent in 2000). Nelson concludes, "Single people and households without children don't want big houses on big lots" (Kiviat 2009: 57–58). Instead, he predicts that they will be attracted to inner-city and first-tier suburban neighborhood amenities, described earlier, that are not commonly available in the outer suburbs and which often have historic roots.

The displacement caused by gentrification and lack of affordable housing has led to the creation of federal programs to address the problem, including the Low Income Tax Credit, New Market Tax Credits, and HUD's HOPE VI. Yet concerns remain as to how exactly to promote revitalization efforts while accommodating lower-income residents.

On the broader municipal scale, the integration of preserving and reusing buildings into sustainability goals aligns well with the goals of the Smart Growth movement. Smart Growth, introduced in chapter 1, is guided by the following principles (SmartGrowth.org 2010):

- Create range of housing opportunities and choices.
- Create walkable neighborhoods.
- Encourage community and stakeholder collaboration.
- Foster distinctive, attractive communities with a strong sense of place.
- Make development decisions predictable, fair, and cost effective.
- Mix land uses.
- Preserve open space, farmland, natural beauty, and critical environmental areas.
- Provide a variety of transportation choices.
- Strengthen and direct development toward existing communities.
- Take advantage of compact building design.

Critics of the smart growth movement saw it as anti-suburb. The Urban Land Institute's *Smart Growth: Myth and Fact* (O'Neill 1999: 6) explained that although 70 percent of Americans wanted to live in suburbs, small towns far from cities, or rural areas, they also wanted a sense of community. But the standard suburbs of the era created social isolation, promoted segregated land uses, fostered a reliance on the automobile, and required long commutes, all of which did not appeal to the discerning home buyer. As a result, many of the most publicized early new urbanist projects such as Seaside, Florida, Kentlands, Maryland, and Celebration, Florida (Shaw and Utt 2000) were established in suburban locations but included some smart growth amenities.

Ironically, the opportunity to acquire large tracts of land commonly associated with these projects presents the impression that smart growth is a suburban opportunity. Much to the contrary, smart growth projects are also located in inner-city neighborhoods and first-tier suburbs and include building rehabilitation, redevelopment, new infill, or a combination of these three in their composition. In 1999, Richard Moe, president of the NTHP, noted that

> Historic preservation is of critical importance to smart growth advocates. By preserving historic structures, towns and cities can revitalize older areas and preserve the uniqueness of their community. In turn, vibrant downtowns, thriving small towns and places that are worth saving reduce our appetite for outward sprawl and new development. (Sierra Club 1999: 22)

This assertion was later supported by David R. Porter, noted growth management consultant and fellow in the Urban Land Institute, who observed,

> Smart growth encourages more growth in urban areas (and less growth in nonurban areas) because growth in urban locations conserves resources, makes efficient use of existing capital assets (building and infrastructure), and adds to the quality of life in metropolitan regions in several ways:
> - Urban locations are highly accessible.
> - Revitalized residential and commercial neighborhoods make distinctive places.
> - The use of existing infrastructure capacity means less construction of new facilities.
> - The revitalization of existing outdoor assets (waterfronts, parks, historic districts, scenic streets) provides recreational opportunities.
> - Important cultural facilities and civic institutions, such as concert halls, museums, and theaters, gain support from a denser population and, in turn, are more readily available to more people. (Porter 2002: 117–118)

Increasing density through repopulation and a greater public interest in returning to the city provide opportunities to live more sustainably. In *Fixing Broken Cities: The Implementation of Urban Development Strategies*, John Kromer, senior consultant for the Fels Institute of Government at the University of Pennsylvania, investigated why people had begun to relocate to urban locations and found the following:

- They believed that urban places had become less blighted and more attractive, cleaner, and safer.
- They enjoyed urban diversity and perceived less threat due to racial and ethnic differences.
- They perceived a variety of educational choices, including magnet schools, charter schools, and well-regarded private and parochial schools.
- They found desirable eating, drinking, entertainment, and shopping choices available day and night.
- They were attracted to new townhouses, lofts, and condominium projects that had been developed on open land and through creative adaptive reuses of architecturally noteworthy former office and industrial buildings.
- Their children had moved on to college and jobs, and their suburban homes were too large and too empty.
- They were bored with the suburbs where they grew up and found the urban environment stimulating.
- They found that urban places were populated by young people passionately engaged in music, art, food, fashion, and politics.
- The suburbs were becoming older and beset with social problems.
- City living was not incompatible with their work, and their jobs were located within a reasonable commuting distance or were Internet facilitated so as to allow them a wider range of residential options (Kromer 2010: 9–10).

There has long been a trend of repurposing former office and warehouse buildings in larger cities for residential use alone or in combination with some commercial use (fig. 2.3). These buildings provide an enormous opportunity for accommodating a growing population in a sustainable manner.

But what about medium and smaller cities and towns that do not have similar building stock to reuse in this manner? For these places, it becomes

Figure 2.3. The successful reuse of existing buildings such as the Denver Dry Goods Building in the LODO district of Denver demonstrated that there is a viable market for these types of residential mixed-use projects in original urban neighborhoods that new urbanism seeks to emulate.

necessary to look at what is already built and investigate the finer grain of the community where repopulation is desired. Because the average house size is shrinking, the existing older building stock may become more attractive to people who seek more sustainable lifestyles and will trade some living space for accessibility to urban living opportunities. These buildings can be reused to foster greater density in communities that demonstrate the advantages of urban living and provide rehabilitation incentives and favorable financing instruments.

   In addition to the development of multitenant housing such as condominium conversions of existing buildings, the creation of new townhouse opportunities, and, as has happened in many cities, the acceptance and legalization of accessory dwelling units (e.g., granny flats, basement apartments), smart growth, and increasing density can be accomplished where land is underused. Three main examples of such underuse are vacant lots, parking lots oversized

for current property usage, and buildings far beyond cost-effective rehabilitation. This does not mean that any deteriorated building should simply be consigned to the landfill, only that economic realities should be observed when
we consider reusing old buildings. Unfortunately, many infill opportunities do
not occur in a contiguous location that enables assemblage of large vacant par-
cels for projects seeking greater economies of scale in construction and marketing. Too often an assemblage of contiguous properties harks back to urban
renewal models where a cleared site was preferred and forced the removal of
buildings that could have been rehabilitated and reused. This stage in the redevelopment process can be recognized when smaller viable but less densely
populated properties are cleared and replaced with new construction (fig. 2.4).
Where protections exist through historic districts or other zoning controls, this
process is more readily monitored. However, contemporary battles are being
fought in unprotected neighborhoods and commercial districts. Those seeking protection through historic register designation and the incentives that accompany that designation align in opposition to those who do not understand
what the designation enables and resent the notions of government oversight
and regulation interfering with their property rights.

Commercial growth tends to lag behind residential growth as retailers want
evidence of viable demand for their products and services. Any revitalization
effort must address the day-to-day needs of the residential repopulation to
improve the prospects of successful commercial repopulation. One approach
has been through the repurposing of urban commercial strip centers where
the departure of a former single large tenant (e.g., a chain grocery store) has
left a vacant building with a large parking lot. Typically built in an era that
looked beyond the immediate local neighborhood and drew customers from a
larger area, these buildings have become expendable as either larger shopping
centers and malls were built elsewhere or the parent company closed local operations. Like their oversized residential counterparts that have been recycled
into commercial uses or multiple-occupancy dwellings, these retail "white el-
ephants" can still be revived, using a variety of techniques mentioned earlier
in this chapter, to serve the emerging local population. With the recognition
that local residents may be less automobile dependent and that smaller units
of local businesses or national chains can be housed in them, owners of these
properties can subdivide the building and infill portions of the parking lot with
new construction (fig. 2.5).

Figure 2.4. These buildings are the outcomes of two cycles of repopulation efforts in the Central City Historic District in Salt Lake City, Utah. The single-family house (center) was an infill project. The new townhouse project (at right) was used to infill a long-vacant lot and included demolishing three other buildings on adjoining lots.

Figure 2.5. In this redeveloped urban retail site, a former grocery store (left background) was subdivided to incorporate smaller retail operations, and a new infill building (right foreground) was constructed in the parking lot to take advantage of the increased population density that has occurred in the Central City Historic District in Salt Lake City, Utah.

The densification of inner-city neighborhoods and first-tier suburbs will continue, but what remains to be seen is how that will occur, whether in replacement of historic vernacular neighborhoods with large, new houses or in a more sensitive, thoughtful development pattern. Certainly, given the available economic incentives and the social and environmental imperatives for increased sustainability, there are opportunities for its success. What will need to happen is a refinement of the broader accessibility to the information on which to base policy decisions and to the tools and metrics used in both early decision making and the subsequent building rehabilitation or construction and operations.

Perspectives from Europe

In the post–World War II era, with European cites devastated by damage from the war, numerous efforts were made to find the best planning strategies to redevelop them into livable communities. In her book *Livable Cities Observed*, Suzanne H. Crowhurst Lennard, director of the International Making Cities Livable Council, noted,

> A consensus emerged in many Western European cities to preserve their historic and visual identity, and to revive—in that process—those essential settings that make possible an enriching and social community life for their inhabitants: public places for markets, for celebrations and entertainment; pedestrian areas for strolling, sitting and meeting people; and residential street environments that limit automobile access. (Crowhurst Lennard and Lennard 1995: 1)

Crowhurst Lennard further observed that the challenge of bringing urban qualities and pleasures of urban social life to larger metropolitan areas and suburbs had eluded European planners, architects, and decision makers as well. She saw that "the failure is most dramatic where the core of the city has remained alive or been dramatically revived." She compared the damage inflicted on cities in wartime Europe with the damage that "was inflicted on the core of [US] cities through ill-advised urban renewal policies, traffic planning priorities, zoning policies, and the construction of single function large-scale commercial centers." Her term for the success of revitalization efforts is *livable*, which recognizes that appropriate urban conservation balances nature in the human habitat. The livability of a city thus depends on the design of human settlements that are in harmony with their landscapes, history, and regional traditions (Crowhurst Lennard and Lennard 1995: 2). The concept of a truly livable city is an engaging goal when that city embraces social, environmental, and economic constructs to ensure sustainability. Although today the list of successes continues to grow throughout Europe, in 1995 Crowhurst Lennard cited several examples where vitality and sustainability were evident at the citywide scale. These included Antwerp, Belgium; Erlangen, Germany; Freiburg-im-Breisgau, Germany; Ravensburg, Germany; and Venice, Italy.

One example that aligns with the principles of stewardship of the built environment is Erlangen, which has gained a reputation as an eco-city. Efforts began in 1972 with the election of mayor Dr. Dietmar Hahlweg. With a population of 100,000 people, Erlangen's success stems from careful attention to traffic and transportation mechanisms (e.g., pedestrian networks, traffic calming, bicycles, public transportation), integrating green into the city (e.g., maintaining green open spaces, planting trees and plants for shade, using pervious paving, which allows percolation of rain into the soil), converting existing industrial buildings into housing, and community participation. The key underlying mechanism was continued public awareness and participation in the planning process. An early recipient of the title *eco-city* in the 1990s, Erlangen continues its efforts to increase its sustainability to this day (Crowhurst Lennard and Lennard 1995; Joss 2009).

The eco-city movement continues to grow worldwide. Although the success stories of Europe are well known, there remains confusion as to how to measure the impact and success of an eco-city and how to avoid the "greenwashing" phenomenon that occurred in early sustainability efforts in individual buildings. As has historically occurred with other metrics, the eco-city movement is supported by a variety of advocacy groups and constituencies, yet their priorities and metrics vary. For example, one nonprofit advocacy group, EcoCity Builders, notes that

An ecocity is an ecologically healthy city. No such city presently exists. We do, however, see hints of ecocities emerging in today's solar, wind and recycling technologies, in green buildings and green businesses, in urban environmental restoration projects, urban gardening and organic farming, and in individuals using foot, bicycle and public modes of transportation in preference to the automobile. (EcoCity Builders 2011)

Their goal is to develop international eco-city standards that will quantify sustainability at the community scale. In defining these standards, the challenge will be to come to a collaborative resolution with other efforts being set forth by *Living Building Challenge, Ecological Performance Standards for Cities,* and the *Natural Step* metric methods being championed by other sustainability advocacy groups (2020climatecampaign 2011), especially in light of the growing recognition of what preserving and reusing buildings can accomplish. The success of this effort will be worth following in the coming decade.

Although a growing minority in the United States recognizes that building preservation and reuse belongs in a larger view of sustainability that extends to the overall cultural landscape, the majority still perceive that new is always better. Thus, steeped in the practices that grew out of a period when the American penchant for new construction and the accompanying tax laws encouraged the removal of existing buildings, the continued focus remains on new construction. Reflecting on European successes in preserving and reusing buildings, Donovan Rypkema, at a Historic Districts Council Annual Conference in New York City on March 10, 2007, made this dour assessment of the American perspective:

> *Much of the world has begun to recognize the interrelationship and the interdependency between sustainable development and heritage conservation; but much less so in the United States.* I'm not so sure we've really learned those lessons in America, or at least we have not yet broadly connected the dots. Far too many advocates in the US far too narrowly define what constitutes sustainable development. Far too many advocates in the US think that so-called green buildings and sustainable development are one in the same. They are not. (Rypkema 2007b)

What remains to be seen is how to facilitate the acceptance of a broader view of stewardship that includes recognizing preservation and reuse as valid constituents of sustainability goals.

Preservation Tools and Processes

A variety of preservation tools and processes are in place that create a framework for effective stewardship. Fully understanding and using these tools appropriately directly affects the societal perception of rehabilitation and adaptive use and how historic preservation practice increases the retention of historic resources. These tools include the following:

- National Register of Historic Places
- Secretary of the Interior Standards
- Design Guidelines
- Main Street Revitalization

National Register of Historic Places (NRHP)

As mentioned earlier, the regulations and laws surrounding the reuse of historically significant buildings present challenges to those unaware of or not fully familiar with them, even as interest in reuse has grown. Historically significant buildings that are eligible for or on the NRHP receive numerous benefits and protections. There are two main areas of confusion. First is the question of what constitutes a historically significant building and, second, when a building is deemed historically significant, what benefits, protections, and regulations apply to it.

The NRHP was established to protect historic resources from adverse effects caused by federally funded projects. Many states, counties, municipalities, and historic societies also maintain historic or cultural registers to identify locally significant resources, which can result in some confusing situations. For example, inclusion on the NRHP does not automatically include an NRHP resource on a local register, nor does placing a resource on a local register automatically include it on the NRHP. Although enabling legislation allows the simultaneous listing on the NRHP and local registers, NRHP resources are added to local registers and come under the attendant oversight only as local ordinances, staffing, and funding allows.

The NRHP is composed of more than 84,000 historic resources (Byrne 2010) that have been deemed historically significant at the national, state, or local level or a combination of the three. These historic resources are classified as follows:

- *Site*: location of a significant event, a prehistoric or historic occupation or activity or a building or structure, whether standing, ruined or vanished, where the location itself possesses historic, cultural, or archeological value regardless of the value of any existing structure
- *Building*: a construction created to shelter any form of human activity
- *Structure*: functional construction made for other than human shelter
- *Object*: construction that is primarily artistic in nature or is small and simply constructed
- *District*: a significant concentration, linkage, or continuity of sites, buildings, structures, or objects united historically or aesthetically by plan or physical development (fig. 2.6)

To list a resource on the NRHP (National Park Service [NPS] 2011b), applicants submit a nomination form that presents supporting evidence about the historic significance of the site, building, structure, object, or district. The primary components of the nomination form include the history of the resource and an analysis of why it is significant and a physical description of the resource and how much of its historic integrity remains from the period of significance. Significance is defined along these four historic criteria:

- Criterion A: events that have made a significant contribution to the broad patterns of our history
- Criterion B: association with the lives of people significant in our past
- Criterion C: embodies distinctive characteristics of a type, period, or method of construction or represents the work of a master, possesses high artistic values, or represents a significant and distinguishable entity whose component may lack individual distinction
- Criterion D: may yield or has already yielded information important to prehistory or history (fig. 2.7)

Figure 2.6. (a) *Site:* Golden Spike National Historic Site, Promontory, Utah; (b) *Building:* Hotel Galvez, Galveston, Texas; (c) *Structure:* Lighthouse, Key West, Florida; (d) *Object:* Zion's First National Bank Clock, Salt Lake City, Utah; and (e) *District:* Utah Circle National Historic District, Salt Lake City, Utah.

a

b

c

d

e

Figure 2.7. Examples of
(a) Criterion A: Antietam
National Military Park;
(b) Criterion B: Henry
Wadsworth Longfellow
House; (c) Criterion C:
Frank Lloyd Wright House
and Studio; (d) Criterion
D: Jamestown National
Historic Site.

a

b

c

d

The State Historic Preservation Office (SHPO) coordinates the NRHP nomination process. Consultations with the SHPO can establish a preliminary finding on the probability of designation. Soon after the SHPO system was established, SHPOs conducted numerous surveys to identify potentially eligible resources. Certain resources were then added to the state and local registers. These surveys usually provide the initial administrative information needed to complete the nomination. The applicant then provides the necessary descriptive and significance details pertaining to the nominated resource.

For historic resources other than districts, the property owner or a preservation consultant can complete the research to determine the historic significance and integrity of the resource. The city planning department, either directly or through a preservation consultant, typically prepares nominations for historic district nomination because the process is more complex due to the greater number of properties involved and the public hearings needed to facilitate completion. All potential historic resources in the proposed district are researched, and once a significance criterion is identified, the resources are categorized as significant, contributing, or noncontributing. The local historic landmarks commission or design review committee uses these designations to determine the level of local protections, if any, that will accrue to the resource. As part of its planning process or at the behest of a citizen's group, the local government typically starts this nomination application process. The applicant holds a series of public workshops, informational planning meetings, and public hearings in which the boundaries and the level of significance for each resource are publicly debated. In all nomination applications, the applicant finalizes the nomination form and submits it to the SHPO, which sends it to the National Park Service regional office for review. When deemed sufficiently complete, it is forwarded to the NRHP for final determination of listing designation.

Listing on or eligibility for the NRHP creates opportunities for numerous funding incentives, especially tax credits, which are increasingly influential in making a project economically feasible. However, listing on or eligibility for the NRHP does not automatically provide local protection unless so enabled by local ordinances and planning department resources. Many property owners fear that designation to the NRHP will limit their personal freedoms in how they modify their buildings. The only protection that NRHP designation implies is mitigation of adverse effects on historic properties by projects using federal funds (e.g., highway projects, urban revitalization programs).

Section 106 of the National Historic Preservation Act of 1966 outlines how to determine adverse effects and how the Advisory Council on Historic Preservation confirms the mitigation of adverse effect. At the most benign level, the person or agency proposing an undertaking that imposes an adverse effect simply withdraws the project or revises it to reduce or eliminate the adverse effect. In the case of a highway project, this could mean realigning a proposed highway improvement to reduce effects on historic resources along the affected section of highway. In a tax credit project, this may mean modifying rehabilitation processes to better conform to the Secretary of the Interior's Guidelines for Rehabilitation.

At the other extreme, the mitigation can entail documenting the historic resource following standards set forth by the Historic American Buildings Survey and then demolishing the historic resource. However, concurrent local designation may provide specific demolition statutes and oversight procedures that must be followed as well.

In addition to or instead of an NRHP listing, local designation introduces oversight by a local historic landmarks commission or design review committee in accordance with locally developed design guidelines. Property owners should verify the designation and oversight status of their properties before commencing work (major exterior alterations, additions, or demolition) that can be viewed from a public way. If there are no local oversight requirements, the property owner is free to proceed in accordance with local zoning and demolition ordinances.

Aside from listing on a local register or NRHP, an alternative level of protection in older neighborhoods that are not part of a historic district is the neighborhood conservation district. This has become an increasingly popular tool to protect the community's character rather than the actual historic fabric. Whereas a historic district has specific guidelines for design review oversight, the conservation district looks more at the underlying development controls. Described as "regulation-lite" historic preservation districts, conservation districts are formed by local governments and specifically protect separate neighborhoods from commercial encroachment or noncompatible infill through attention to such things as permitted uses; streetscapes; density and floor area ratio requirements; building massing, height, and setback; signage; and off-street parking and loading requirements (Stipe 2003: 141–142; Miller 2004). Conservation districts are particularly useful when insufficient public support exists for the oversight of a historic district.

Secretary of the Interior's Standards

In the hierarchy of the federal government, the secretary of the interior administers the National Park Service and has ultimate responsibility for preservation activities pertaining to government interests. To promote an understanding of the preservation principles that are applied to *historic properties*, the secretary of the interior has defined four treatments: preservation, rehabilitation, restoration, and reconstruction. The distinction between them deals with how original materials are preserved or reconstructed:

- Preservation focuses on the maintenance and repair of existing historic materials and retention of a property's form as it has evolved over time.
- Rehabilitation acknowledges the need to alter or add to an historic property to meet continuing or changing uses while retaining the property's historic character.
- Restoration depicts a property at a particular period of time in its history, while removing evidence of other periods.
- Reconstruction re-creates vanished or non-surviving portions of a property for interpretive purposes. (NPS 2011d)

The recommended practices for *rehabilitation* are the most commonly used, so the following discussion focuses on that treatment.

The *Secretary of the Interior's Standards* were developed pursuant to the goals of the Venice Charter of 1966 and published in 1976 to codify how alterations undertaken to accommodate contemporary demands could include sensitivity toward protecting and retaining the historic character-defining features of historic properties. The Standards for Rehabilitation are as follows:

1. A property shall be used for its historic purpose or be placed in a new use that requires minimal change to the defining characteristics of the building and its site and environment.
2. The historic character of a property shall be retained and preserved. The removal of historic materials or alteration of features and spaces that characterize a property shall be avoided.
3. Each property shall be recognized as a physical record of its time, place, and use. Changes that create a false sense of historical development, such as adding conjectural features or architectural elements from other buildings, shall not be undertaken.

4. Most properties change over time; those changes that have acquired historic significance in their own right shall be retained and preserved.

5. Distinctive features, finishes, and construction techniques or examples of craftsmanship that characterize a property shall be preserved.

6. Deteriorated historic features shall be repaired rather than replaced. Where the severity of deterioration requires replacement of a distinctive feature, the new feature shall match the old in design, color, texture, and other visual qualities and, where possible, materials. Replacement of missing features shall be substantiated by documentary, physical, or pictorial evidence.

7. Chemical or physical treatments, such as sandblasting, that cause damage to historic materials shall not be used. The surface cleaning of structures, if appropriate, shall be undertaken using the gentlest means possible.

8. Significant archeological resources affected by a project shall be protected and preserved. If such resources must be disturbed, mitigation measures shall be undertaken.

9. New additions, exterior alterations, or related new construction shall not destroy historic materials that characterize the property. The new work shall be differentiated from the old and shall be compatible with the massing, size, scale, and architectural features to protect the historic integrity of the property and its environment.

10. New additions and adjacent or related new construction shall be undertaken in such a manner that if removed in the future, the essential form and integrity of the historic property and its environment would be unimpaired. (Morton et al. 1992: vi–vii)

Design Guidelines

First published in 1977, the *Secretary of the Interior's Guidelines for Rehabilitation* were developed by the secretary of the interior "to help property owners, developers, and Federal managers apply the *Secretary of the Interior's Standards* during the project planning stage by providing general design and technical recommendations" (Morton et al. 1992: viii). The *Guidelines* pertain to the building exterior and interior, the site, the overall setting, energy conservation, new additions, and accessibility, health, and safety. They present procedural recommendations on how to identify, retain, and preserve; protect and maintain; repair; replace; and design for missing historic features. The categories are further divided in recommended and not recommended practices. For an example of the typical format for the *Guidelines*, see http://www.nps.gov/hps/tps/standguide/preserve/preserve_masonry.htm.

The *Guidelines* are the primary basis for many local design guides and, by and large, form the fundamental basis for appropriate preservation practice. As with the *Standards*, local design guidelines pertain to historic buildings that are under the review of local government. They provide insights into the sensitivity expected in historic districts but for nonhistoric buildings, but they are tied to the ordinances covering zoning (e.g., permitted uses, setbacks, height limits), demolition, and signage. This has been a fundamental source of friction for residents of older neighborhoods that, though perhaps eligible for protection, remain unprotected and thus create opportunities for construction of "monster" homes. Recognition of this threat can prompt local residents to pursue local historic district status. When a local district is formed, the local government typically adopts a set of design guidelines (developed by them or by a preservation consultant) that are specifically attuned to that district. The development of guidelines varies nationwide, but content often reflects the format of the secretary's delineation of guidelines. (Note: For various examples of design guidelines, visit http://www.uga.edu/napc/programs/napc/guidelines.htm).

Although design guidelines are not uniform throughout the country, they share an overarching goal: to retain the historic character-defining features that can be seen from a public way. The guidelines provide direction to property owners, designers, contractors, and public officials as to what is deemed appropriate. Other common goals include the following:

- *Architectural research and archival research*: Investigate on site and in archives to identify historic character-defining features.
- *Historic fabric retention*: Keep character-defining features (ornament, construction assemblies, finishes, and fixtures).
- *Sensitive additions*: Ensure that new additions do not obscure the historic appearance.
- *Avoidance of false history*: Ensure that alterations stand of their own time and are differentiated from the original construction.
- *Sensitive changes for accessibility*: Provide accessibility without harming historic fabric.

- *Appropriate window replacement*: Ensure that windows appropriately match original window size and profile.
- *Appropriate materials*: Promote the use of materials that are compatible with the historic character defining features.
- *Reversible treatments*: Use treatments that can be reversed without damage.

The guidelines follow criteria based on the context cues of the specific district. This means that any alterations, additions, or new construction must include attention to such cues as height, width, and setback; massing; proportion of openings; horizontal rhythms; roof form; and material palette. In addition, other features covered in design guidelines may include signage, pedestrian orientation, vehicle circulation, and parking (figs. 2.8 and 2.9).

Recent guidelines pay more attention to how to accommodate sustainability. The key debate is that alterations that affect the visual coherence of a building should be given care in the decision processes. The secretary of the interior

Figure 2.8. Height, width, and setback; massing; proportion of openings; horizontal rhythms; roof form; and material palette create the basis for the context analysis used to create design guidelines. Other aspects covered may address signage, pedestrian orientation, vehicle circulation, and parking. Shown here is part of the 25th Street Historic District in Ogden, Utah.

Figure 2.9. Well-formulated preservation ordinances, design guidelines, and demolition ordinances can prevent the loss of historic resources and prevent incompatible infill. This Rite-Aid Drugstore in Camden, Maine demonstrates compatible infill.

has recognized the implications that demands for implementing sustainability measures will have on historic buildings and released *The Secretary of the Interior's Standards for Rehabilitation & Illustrated Guidelines on Sustainability for Rehabilitating Historic Buildings* in 2011 to address the following issues:

- Sustainability
- Planning
- Maintenance
- Windows
- Weatherization and insulation
- Heating, ventilating, and air conditioning and air circulation
- Solar technology
- Wind power (wind turbines and windmills)
- Roofs (cool roofs and green roofs)
- Site features and water efficiency
- Daylighting (Grimmer, Hensley, Petrella, and Tepper 2011)

These guidelines clarify how older and historic buildings may already include sustainability features and how to appropriately integrate new ones into them. The *Sustainability Guidelines* form a necessary adjunct to the other *Secretary of the Interior's Guidelines* because the *Standards* and these other *Guidelines* already inform the fundamental process that many local governments and agencies use for design review.

Perhaps the most common debate is over replacement windows: whether it is economically feasible to repair existing windows, when they should be replaced, and what new material should be used. Evidence has shown that the perception of how effective (or not) new replacement windows can be is an ongoing point of misunderstanding and contention. Other approaches to sustainability that are being increasingly used in new construction have been the focus of contentious debate in retrofits of existing buildings with historic value: wind generation systems, photovoltaic panels, solar panels, and other renewable forms of energy generation. Specifically, the use of solar and photovoltaic panels has charged this debate in historic districts because these products and other materials may conflict with rehabilitation design guidelines developed before sustainability became a recognized issue. Traditionally, these objects could have been installed only where they would not be seen from a public way. However, a conflict arises when property owners want to install them on the primary façades or roof. The question may even become moot at the local level because, as preservation planning consultant Noré Winter notes in *Developing Sustainability Guidelines for Historic Districts* (Winter 2011: 11–12),

> Some commissions may permit solar panels to be more visible, using the argument that they can be interpreted as "later alterations," when the historic character of the resource can still be understood. This may be a factor where local governments encourage high visibility of solar retrofits in order to promote their use.

The incipient problem arises, however, when the property owners of these same locally approved installations subsequently apply for the assorted federal tax credit programs for preservation and energy conservation. Because any project involving federal funding that affects a building on or eligible for the NRHP must confirm compliance with the *Standards* and their accompanying guidelines, there is the possibility that these installations may be rejected at

the federal review level. This will no doubt add greater confusion and con-
sternation in the future sustainability enhancement efforts that will need to be
resolved at both local and federal review levels. Without this resolution, public
confidence in the value of preservation as a sustainability strategy will erode.

Main Street Redevelopment

In the 1970s, the NTHP recognized the difficulties that local governments
and community groups in smaller cities and towns were having in revitalizing
commercial business districts. The NTHP created the National Main Street
Center (NMSC) in 1980 to assist in these local efforts. The NMSC provides
training programs and technical assistance for Main Street "managers" and
their constituencies. The NMSC has developed the "Main Street Approach,"
which consists of four points that should be incorporated into a successful
program:

- *Organization*: Identify and organize the stakeholders in the community whose assistance will be instrumental in making the revitalization
  successful.
- *Promotion*: Identify and promote the market niches that will help attract
  people to the downtown.
- *Design*: Identify and capitalize on the design qualities of existing building stock that gives the downtown its unique character.
- *Economic restructuring*: Identify economic factors and opportunities that
  can improve the economic structure of the town.

A review of successful Main Street communities revealed that they demonstrate the following characteristics:

- *Comprehensive*: No single focus can revitalize Main Street.
- *Incremental*: Successful revitalization programs begin with basic, simple
  activities that demonstrate that "new things are happening" in the commercial district.
- *Self-help*: Leaders must have the will and desire to mobilize local resources and talent.
- *Partnerships*: Both the public and private sectors have a vital interest in
  the district and must work together to achieve common goals of Main
  Street's revitalization.

- *Identifying and capitalizing on existing assets*: Business districts must capitalize on the assets that make them unique: distinctive buildings and human scale that give people a sense of belonging.
- *Quality*: Emphasize quality in every aspect of the revitalization program, from storefront designs to promotional campaigns to educational programs.
- *Change*: Changes in attitude and practice are slow but definite; public support for change will build as the Main Street program grows and consistently meets its goals.
- *Implementation*: Main Street must show visible results that can come only from completing projects (NMSC 2010a).

Community stakeholders form an independent nonprofit agency and hire a Main Street manager, trained in the Main Street approach, to coordinate efforts. The NMSC has assisted more than 1,600 communities over the past 25 years (NMSC 2010d) and currently lists more than 1,300 communities actively working in forty states and the District of Columbia (NMSC 2010c). The success of this program bodes well as a touchstone for what can be accomplished when the holistic view of reusing and preserving buildings is included in the discussion and execution of a revitalization plan. Its expected long-term success will bode well as an iconic example of how stewardship of the built environment can increase sustainability.

Sociopolitical Framework

The growth of the historic preservation movement has been marked by several compounding forces that have occurred unevenly across the country:

- The perception that preservation is anti-progressive
- Laws and statutes that provide multiple and potentially concurrent paths of oversight from local, state, and federal agencies
- Issues of perceived civil liberties infringement
- Myths and misconceptions that arise from these other forces

First, early efforts toward preservation were often met with resistance from parties promoting "progress and growth." The prevailing sentiment was that saving the old impeded the possibilities of a successful new. Preservationists were characterized as anti-progressive, and they often appealed for support through nostalgia and emotional attachment to the historic resource in question. Fortunately, the preservation movement has matured and broadened to recognize the economic and environmental ramifications of retaining buildings, as demonstrated by the NTHP Main Street Program and the many federal, state, and local financial incentives available. The ever-increasing number of successful preservation and adaptive use projects demonstrate positive outcomes in social, environmental, and economic terms.

Second, although the framework for the process has been well defined in its original formation, the subtle localized variations in actual processes often remain unclear to the uninformed public or inexperienced designer, contractor, property owner, or public official. This lack of clarity and intent can create unnecessary conflict and antagonism when everyone involved does not understand how the process works. The best approach is to directly investigate the implications of oversight in each particular place and situation.

The plan review and building permit processes for alterations to nonhistoric buildings are well understood in general practice. However, proposed alterations to a building on a local, state, or national historic register can trigger additional layers of oversight and review. For buildings designated only at the local level, this review is performed by the local historic landmarks commission, which issues a certificate of appropriateness based on adherence to local design guidelines. When properties are listed on or eligible for the NRHP, any projects that use federal funds (e.g., tax credits) will trigger further review.

In addition to the federal laws, state and local municipalities enact additional laws and statutes that meet the specific demands of their local population. With the laws and regulations coming from three sources—each with a possibly different perspective—interpretations and place-specific origins at the local level have led to many disputes over land use and who actually had oversight and regulatory responsibility, as well as misperceptions and myths about the restrictions imposed by preservation. Oversight requirements for grants, loans, building performance rating systems, and other incentive programs can add more confusion. To make matters worse, the requirements or allowances of these programs can often conflict with the requirements of the other programs. For example, a local design guideline may allow a greater range of materials or practices than are allowed under the federal historic tax credit guidelines. For instance, the owners of two similar residential buildings in the same historic district may seek to replace the roofing. Homeowner A obtains approval through the local landmarks commission to obtain a certificate of appropriateness to use a simulated slate shingle that is acceptable under local guidelines. Homeowner B also decides to replace his roof with the same product but wants to apply for the historic tax credits, which will be further reviewed through the State Historic Preservation Office and the National Park Service. Unbeknownst to Homeowner B, this particular type of shingle is not accepted under the *Secretary of the Interior's Standards for Rehabilitation*, and he is told that these otherwise locally acceptable shingles are not appropriate. Homeowner B is also told that he must use a different shingle that is accepted under the *Standards* to obtain the tax credit. This point of confusion stems from the fact that although most local design guidelines are based on the *Standards*, local landmarks commissions may evolve their interpretation based on local precedents created as a result of the local conditions.

As a consequence of these two forces, a third force comes into play when property owners claim infringement on their personal civil liberties and property rights and take measures (e.g., lawsuits and threats of lawsuits or other methods of intimidation) to "protect" them. Unfortunately for preservationists, these are the cases that commonly gain local news media attention. This negative, misinformed coverage can discourage innovative and creative solutions for preserving and reusing the built environment. Property owners, developers, lending institutions, and municipal leaders dismiss rehab or preservation projects as too difficult or too financially risky and look to develop where oversight is less strict, or choose to rely on demolition of existing buildings to clear a site for the "new" project.

Designation of historic districts and enactment of local regulations occur through a public hearing process in which every citizen has an opportunity to voice his or her concerns. Historic designation and acceptance of oversight that accompanies such a designation represents the will of the majority of people living within the affected properties. In light of their recognized contribution to the public good, historic preservation regulations and processes have been deemed constitutional by the US Supreme Court. As a result, innumerable instances have occurred in which a successful preservation outcome was achieved through the collaborative efforts between property owners, designers, contractors, and the municipalities who are facilitating private demands while acting in the public interest.

Perhaps the single most vexing aspect of design review is that in many instances, the character-defining features included in design guidelines for local design reviews may vary between districts in the same community. Because of the evolution in how and when districts were deemed significant (and without preexisting general overlay guidelines covering all districts), historic districts designated in a community may have differing characteristics that are uniquely identified in the statement of significance in their historic register nomination. In certain instances, earlier districts may include broader or narrower protections than later districts, based on the varying level of detail of architectural research conducted in preparing the nomination. For example, the statement of significance that identifies character-defining features in one district may include outbuildings, structures, and landscape features (e.g., carriage houses, gazebos, arbors, and fencing) that are visible from a public way, whereas the statement of significance for another district may address only the primary buildings and streetscape. This inconsistency often is revealed by a statement such as "My friend lives in ABC District and was allowed to do XYZ. I thought I could do that where I live (in JKL District) too."

Although comprehensive uniformity would simplify many issues in preservation, the political and economic realities of uniformly identifying and reassessing character-defining features in earlier or later districts limits this. In numerous cases, the concept of uniform design guidelines for all districts emerges only after several have been designated, thereby making the creation of a uniform design guideline retroactively extremely difficult. Although community leaders can develop certain procedural provisions for community-wide application, each individual district retains its own specific provisions. Property owners should verify the oversight status and guidelines pertaining to their properties before commencing work (e.g., major exterior alterations, additions, or demolition). If there are no local oversight requirements, the property owner is free to proceed in accordance with local zoning, permitting, and demolition ordinances.

Collaborative Practice

Rehabilitation and adaptive use of the built environment can be complex and nearly indecipherable for those unfamiliar with the regulatory, social, and technical processes involved. There are many opportunities and constraints (which is which depends on your perspective) to completing a building rehabilitation or adaptive use project, and these multiply as the scale of the project increases from a building to a neighborhood or commercial business district. Although each city or town has its own interpretation of the overall process, a survey of housing developers in Atlanta reveals some common barriers to undertaking urban redevelopment projects:

- High land costs
- Neighborhood opposition
- Complex zoning and permitting processes
- Inflexible zoning restrictions and regulations
- The need to design new projects to fit into existing neighborhoods
- High cost of deck parking for high-density projects
- Lack of popular and market support for and knowledge of higher-density and mixed use projects (Porter 2002: 130)

These become further complicated when the requirements of historic district oversight, government incentive programs, financial institutions, and high performance building standards are added to the mix. But don't be discouraged!

To minimize risk, architects are increasingly moving toward collaborative practice to better address requirements and facilitate the successful completion of the project. This often means forming temporary partnerships between firms in the design and construction industry. These partnerships traditionally exist for the duration of the project planning, design, and construction periods. With recent demand for building commissioning, this partnership often extends through that period as well. Each firm and consultant retains its separate internal structure, but together the partnership emulates the activities of a much larger, more sophisticated organization with broader and deeper levels of expertise.

For smaller projects, such as a single-family home, these parties may be included in the process directly or indirectly, through the expertise of the architectural facilitator (architect, designer, contractor, or even the homeowner). In a large-scale project, the various parties are more likely to be directly engaged. At either extreme, the more successful projects are those that have open communications and information flow between all the parties (fig. 2.10).

Figure 2.10. Collaborative planning, design, and construction management practices used at Fort Douglas in Salt Lake City, Utah enabled the conversion of this decommissioned army base into a "Living and Learning Community" that includes dorms, academic offices, and research centers for the University of Utah. This also was the site of the athletes' village for the 2002 Winter Olympics.

Connecting the Dots

Even in this complex oversight and regulatory environment, there have been many successful preservation and adaptive reuse projects in the past three decades. Although there are still many challenges to overcome, the successes give rise to hope that they are repeatable. These challenges include cost control, risk aversion, and a lack of understanding about how preserving and reusing an existing building can be sustainable. The forces that drive decision making about building construction still move away from reusing buildings and create significant resistance to a fully comprehensive vision of the spectrum of sustainable processes. With the ongoing success in European models of building reuse and the emerging ecodistrict movement in North America, there is an opportunity to further strengthen the socially conscious realization of how sustainable reusing buildings can be.

In the 5-year period since Rypkema's assessment, there has been a ground-swell toward connecting the dots. In addition to ongoing research and edu-cational efforts of the United Nations Educational, Scientific and Cultural Organization's International Centre for the Study of the Preservation and Res-toration of Cultural Property in Europe, the Getty Conservation Institute in the United States, and the many national and academic centers worldwide fo-cusing on building conservation practices, there is an emerging recognition of the need to bring the sustainability aspects of reusing buildings (both historic and nonhistoric) into mainstream conversation on green building and sustain-able design. The increasingly broad acceptance of many preservation and reuse projects nationwide as attractive and livable communities stands as testament to the social success of these projects. As the research findings of Arthur C. Nel-son portend, there is and will continue to be growing demand for an enhanced urban environment in which social interactions, walkability, and automobile independence are the increasingly expected social norms. These amenities are readily achievable within the existing built environment of the inner city and first-tier suburbs of the early twentieth century. Furthermore, as the Preserva-tion Green Lab (2012: 17–18) notes, many of these older buildings also in-clude characteristics of passive design and passive survivability that allow use of the building without energy inputs that can happen during power failures.

The NTHP is one organization that is leading this shift through programs such as the National Main Street Center and, more recently, its Preservation Green Lab (PGL). Established in 2009 in Seattle, Washington, PGL explores the relationships between preservation and sustainability and the continued livability of cities. As described on its website, PGL's mission includes de-veloping and promoting "strategic policies for integrating the reuse and ret-rofitting of older and historic buildings into city and state efforts to reduce greenhouse gas emissions and achieve other sustainability objectives" (NTHP 2011a). When asked what lessons she hoped elected officials, local developers, local decision makers, and the general public would learn from the PGL and its initiatives, Liz Dunn, consulting director of PGL, responded,

> I hope they learn that the reasons for preserving our existing building stock aren't strictly cultural and sentimental; preservation should be understood as a land-use tool and as an economic tool that can be used to build denser, more attractive cities. I think the general public gets this at a gut level, perhaps more

than the policy-makers and the developers. Fundamentally, what we want policy-makers to learn is that their automatic reaction should be "Why should we throw this building away?" rather than "Why should we keep it?" (NTHP 2011c)

PGL has thus initiated two major policy projects that may transform how existing buildings and communities are made more sustainable. These projects include exploring outcome-based codes and district energy. Although it is commonly known that existing buildings consume significant amounts of energy, the prescriptive energy codes used today do not encourage their retrofit. The one-size-fits-all approach ignores the strengths and weaknesses of individual buildings and can create obstacles for rehabilitating buildings by requiring modifications that can adversely affect historic character-defining features and reduce their value. Moreover, conventional energy codes lag behind new approaches to energy reduction.

These approaches cannot adequately recognize whole-building strategies that link passive thermal systems with on-site renewable energy generation or low-carbon district energy systems. PGL proposes using an outcome-based approach to retrofits, so owners can pursue the strategies they deem appropriate to their building. The tradeoff is that they would need to meet a pre-negotiated performance target. As the next step beyond smart building codes, outcome-based codes would influence tenant behavior and could become a significant tool in promoting human activity that lessens the environmental impact of buildings. Because of the implications for national applicability and the potential to catalyze widespread change, PGL is working with the City of Seattle to test new code concepts and inform development of a model code ordinance. In doing so, PGL and the New Buildings Institute brought together energy performance policy makers in Washington and British Columbia to inform Seattle's model ordinance. The expectation is that Seattle's ordinance will provide an example for other cities and also influence national energy code standards such as the International Green Construction Code (NTHP 2011c). The efforts of the PGL have already gained notice. In January 2011, the Earth Advantage Institute, a nonprofit green building resource and research organization that has certified more than eleven thousand sustainable homes, included outcome-based codes in its top ten green building trends for 2011 (Earth Advantage Institute 2011).

PGL has recognized that although outcome-based code work will help individual buildings achieve aggressive energy targets, many older and historic buildings will not achieve net zero energy usage without on-site renewable energy generation or access to low-carbon district energy systems. Therefore, the other major PGL policy project has been exploring ways to improve the use of district energy and utility service production. The concept, already historically used in major cities to provide district heating and cooling in their central business district core, is simply the centralization of energy production and transformation facilities such that existing buildings can access the benefits of renewable energy resources without constructing those facilities on site. As described by PGL, district energy systems are

> neighborhood-scale utilities that are specifically created and financed to deliver energy services—including heating, cooling, and hot water—to a collection of buildings within a defined service area. They are able to deliver energy from a variety of alternative low-carbon sources such as biomass, recaptured waste heat, geothermal, and ground source heat pumps. Low-carbon district energy can play a vital role in enabling existing buildings to meet increasingly aggressive emission reduction targets in a cost-effective and energy-efficient way. (NTHP 2011c)

PGL has partnered with the University of Oregon's Center for Sustainable Business Practices to create a primer for sustainability policy makers and local government officials that explains the importance of district energy nationwide. The final publication, "The Role of District Energy in Greening Existing Neighborhoods" (Osdoba and Dunn 2010), explores in detail how district energy can be a critical element of successful community energy plans for existing neighborhoods. It provides examples from around North America to show various strategies for success and the crucial role of city governments in promoting and implementing district energy (NTHP 2001c).

Congruous with the intent of district energy, the ecodistrict concept has been gaining favor nationwide. As delineated by the Portland Sustainability Institute (POSI), an ecodistrict is "a neighborhood or district with a broad commitment to accelerate neighborhood-scale sustainability" (POSI 2012). Originally conceived and successfully completed in several European cities in the late twentieth century, these ecological urban renewal projects or urban regeneration projects have provided significant precedence for North America. Albeit smaller than at the full citywide scale that has emerged in Europe as a result of years of fine-tuning, the ecodistrict could be the starting point for sustainability efforts in any community in that retaining buildings can provide a connection to the sense of place that begets that community. New construction becomes the infill between existing buildings, which connect to the overall sense of place and build on the community's values and traditions. In Europe, some notable ones that include the preservation and reuse of buildings can be found at Fredensgade, Kolding, Denmark; Solgarden, Kolding, Denmark; Unionplatz, Berlin, Germany; Block 103, Berlin, Germany; Bijlmermeer, Amsterdam, The Netherlands; and Augustenburg, Malmö, Sweden.

As urban sustainability scholar Timothy Beatley notes, "The urban regenerative project at Fredensgade in Kolding is one of the most spectacular ecological urban renewal projects." This project included 140 flats within four- and five-story buildings that were creatively renovated and integrated with a number of ecological elements such as a centralized greenhouse, significant building envelope upgrades, rainwater capture, photovoltaics, and solar panels (Beatley 2000: 304–306; Beatley 2004: 136).

Ecodistricts are emerging in the United States, most notably in Portland, Oregon. Portland has already gained acclaim for its efforts to reuse individual buildings in meaningful ways (e.g., Gerding Theater, Ecotrust Headquarters) and redevelop entire neighborhoods (e.g., the Pearl District) that retain the historic attributes that contribute to the overall social sustainability of the city. The introduction of ecodistricts is a natural extension of these efforts to consolidate a vision of sustainability on a city scale and highlight what adhering to the principles of stewardship can achieve. POSI's Ecodistrict Initiative notes that approaches to improving neighborhood sustainability (e.g., energy and water management systems, green streets, and resource conservation) are well known. Conversely, the *Ecodistrict Initiative* also recognizes that their broader implementation has been hindered by inadequate "comprehensive assessment tools, scalable project capital, and public policy support." The *Ecodistrict Initiative* strives to eliminate these barriers and devise strategies to increase sustainability at the neighborhood level (POSI 2012). Here again, Liz Dunn notes in an interview for *Metropolis Magazine* that the ecodistrict movement has been fueled by the realization that when neighborhood-scale investments are made, the resulting aggregation is "how those neighborhoods full of great old buildings—the ones that are attracting people back into cities—will get to top energy performance" (Levitt 2010).

Based on these initiatives and the numerous others around the country, it appears as though the United States is beginning to connect the dots on a local level. Although the European (and worldwide) ecocity movement has outpaced the United States, efforts such as the ecodistrict initiative indicate that we are creating the foundation for greater advances in both the short and the long term. As Richard Register, founder of Urban Ecology and Ecocity Builders, notes in his book *Ecocities*, one approach is to start anywhere you can and systematically build up from there (Register 2006: 327). The coming decade should realize the maturation of these efforts as their outcomes become more broadly published and well known and can therefore serve as models for the development of similar or expanded efforts throughout the country.

As shown in this chapter, the means and methods are available that contribute to the social success of the preservation and adaptive use of the built environment. There are many interpretations of what they mean. These interpretations and misperceptions form the public opinion about what preservation entails. This lack of clarity continues to cloud the vision for many people. For those who understand the system and can manage within it, their outcomes provide evidence of how it works in the contemporary social context. Those who do not understand the procedures and policies often run afoul of the oversight involved and have less successful outcomes.

Using the European precedents and early North American examples as a starting point and continuing to demonstrate how these concepts work, advocates for the appropriate stewardship of the built environment can continue to gain momentum in their efforts to bring a more comprehensive understanding of how building preservation and reuse is part of sustainable design.

The level of complexity increases dramatically as broader sociopolitical aspects of reusing an existing urban core are considered. Although these sociopolitical opportunities and constraints provide numerous venues for progress, and the overall task may seem daunting, the growing number of success stories, preserving and reusing buildings as part of recognized sustainability strategy continues to move toward mainstream acceptance. This will not happen overnight, but growing evidence indicates that it is achievable.

CHAPTER THREE
Environmental Factors

The evolution of building construction practices throughout the twentieth century has left a spectrum of good and bad practices that architects, engineers, contractors, planners, civic officials, and property owners must recognize to facilitate their efforts to achieve sustainability. Changes in architectural building technologies, particularly in the period after World War II, led to dramatic shifts in how buildings were designed, built, and operated. The nascent passive solar energy movement coupled with the two energy crises of the 1970s that prompted dramatic energy cost increases and heightened concerns over energy security led to a different way to view building performance. Building designers seemed to take note of these lessons and began to design more energy-efficient buildings.

Fuel prices and availability stabilized in the 1980s yet still remain high compared with those of the pre-crisis period. However, uncertainty in fuel cost escalation creates growing concerns over energy security and the long-term sustainability of buildings. The numerous energy retrofits completed in the 1980s revealed that there were many alternative solutions to reducing energy use, some of which translate directly from constructing new buildings to retrofitting existing ones. The techniques that translated well included upgrading operational and control aspects of mechanical, electrical, plumbing, and lighting systems with more energy-efficient replacement products or control overlays programmed to use less energy. Modifications to the building envelope that emulated new building construction led to adding insulation to walls and roofs and infilling windows with insulated panels or replacing them altogether. Unfortunately, in certain instances the cost of removing preexisting envelope components, such as windows, made the proposed strategy cost-prohibitive.

Decision makers started paying greater attention to energy payback periods and specifically kept first costs to a minimum and focused on recovering the cost of more incrementally expensive design alternatives through the expected energy savings alone. These analysis methods have since been supplemented and even surpassed through the use of life cycle analysis software and databases.

At this same time, design professionals began to recognize the inherent sustainability present in many of the features common to buildings built before the mid-1950s. Initial attempts to conserve energy by infilling windows with materials designed to resist heat loss often resulted in higher electrical lighting costs because they blocked daylight. Studies began to reveal that the long-forgotten or overlooked strategies of using thermal mass to moderate temperature swings or taking advantage of natural ventilation could play an important role in energy performance. The more thermally massive buildings built before World War II had different operating characteristics than the less thermally massive curtain wall of the post–World War II era. These and other characteristics of architectural form and tectonics are discussed in further detail in this chapter.

This chapter begins with an examination of how environmental indicators apply to existing buildings as metrics for performance. Then it explores the opportunities and constraints that existing buildings place on efforts to achieve sustainability. The chapter concludes with an exploration of current environmental trends that provide opportunities to improve stewardship of the built environment.

Environmental Indicators

In addition to Leadership in Energy and Environmental Design (LEED), several other quantification systems are available worldwide. The US Environmental Protection Agency and the US Department of Energy developed Energy Star (USEPA-USDOE 2011) in 1992 to originally assess various appliances and by 1995 had expanded the program to include businesses and homes. Although LEED has dominated the market, Energy Star is a complementary system that is gaining broader use. Two other programs, the Building Research Establishment Environmental Assessment Method (BREEAM 2011) and the Green Building Initiative's Green Globes (Green Building Initiative 2011), respectively developed in the United Kingdom and Canada, have gained an international following.

Designers and analysts compare the environmental performance of various buildings at a comprehensive scale or the potential benefits of various alternative design options. Several environmental indicators are commonly used to measure building performance. These include the energy utilization index (EUI), embodied energy invested in existing buildings, material flows from raw materials to landfill wastes, and life cycle analysis.

Energy Utilization Index

The EUI measures energy use by taking the sum of the total energy usage for heating, cooling, lighting, and electrical plug loads for the study period (typically 1 year) divided by the gross area of the building. This is expressed in kilo–British thermal units (kBtu). Some analysts express the EUI in British thermal units per square foot, so you must pay attention to the units being used when comparing different projects. Thus, the EUI formula becomes

EUI (kBtu/sf) = Total energy usage (kBtu)/Gross building area (sf).

When more than one fuel is used, convert each source total to kilo–British thermal units (box 3.1) and then add them together to find the total energy use. The results give a relative indication of the energy use profile that can be used to assess the general energy performance of buildings of different sizes or construction periods. The following examples illustrate how the EUI is determined.

EXAMPLE 1

Find the EUI of a 16,000-square-foot building that uses only electricity for heating, cooling, and lighting and has used a total of 481,500 kwh.

SOLUTION

The first step is to convert the kilowatt hours to kilo–British thermal units by using the conversion factor 3.412 kBtu/kwh:

Total energy usage = 481,500 × 3.412 = 1,642,878 kBtu.

The second step is to divide the result by the gross square footage of the building to obtain the EUI:

EUI = 1,642,878/16,000 sf = 102.7 kBtu/sf.

Box 3.1

Energy Conversion Factors

To calculate an EUI in kilo–British thermal units (kBtu), multiply each fuel source total by the relevant conversion factor:

Fuel	Factor (kBtu)
Anthracite coal (lb)	14.6
No. 2 oil (gal)	141.0
Natural gas (ccf)	105.0
Propane (cf)	2.5
Electricity (kwh)	3.412
Wood (lb)	7.0

Source: Abstracted from Stein et al. (2010: 259).

EXAMPLE 2

Find the EUI of a 20,000-square-foot building that uses electricity and natural gas for heating, cooling, and lighting. The total electrical consumption is 244,000 kwh. The total gas consumption is 12,000 therms.

SOLUTION

The first step is to determine the kilo–British thermal units used by each fuel by using the conversion factor 3.412 kBtu/kwh:

Electrical consumption = 244,000 × 3.412 = 832,528 kBtu.

Convert the therms to kilo–British thermal units by using the conversion factor 100 kBtu/therm:

Natural gas consumption = 8,000 × 100 = 800,000 kBtu.

Next, add them together to find the total kilo–British thermal units consumed:

Total consumption = 832,528 + 800,000 = 1,632,528 kBtu.

The final step is to divide the kilo–British thermal units used by the gross square footage of the building to obtain the EUI:

EUI = 1,632,528/20,000 sf = 81.6 kBtu/sf.

The EUI is an important metric to compare buildings. In a study released by the US Department of Energy in 2008 (table 3.1), the energy-intensive modernist buildings of the 1960s and 1970s are shown to be poor performers; however, it is the commercial buildings built in the 1980s, after two energy crises, that are the worst performers of the past half century. Furthermore, the post-1990 EUIs and the pre-1920s and 1950s EUIs are extremely similar. More telling is the fact that the post-2000 buildings exhibit an EUI that is only 0.6 percent better than that of commercial buildings built before 1920. This illustrates that pre-1920s buildings are already nearly as energy efficient as buildings constructed in the early twenty-first century, and, by extension, they have many design characteristics worth emulating in future designs. This also shows that the buildings of the late twentieth century face the biggest challenges in achieving energy efficiency because of their primary reliance on mechanical and electrical systems to achieve comfort.

Several factors can explain these variations in EUI. First, many of the buildings built before 1920 were constructed of heavier masonry materials that provided thermal mass, included natural ventilation strategies for cooling, and

Table 3.1
Average Energy Consumption (in kBtu/sf) for
Commercial Buildings (Excluding Malls)

Before 1920	80.2
1920–1945	90.3
1946–1959	80.3
1960–1969	90.9
1970–1979	95.0
1980–1989	100.1
1990–1999	88.8
2000–2003	79.7

US Department of Energy (2008).

relied a great deal on daylighting. Although invented in the early twentieth century, air conditioning did not become widely used until after World War II. Fluorescent lamps and double-paned windows were introduced in the 1930s, and the aluminum curtain wall gained greater use in the 1950s and beyond. Their use transformed buildings as operable windows, atria, thermal mass, and other pre-1920 standard design elements disappeared from the mid-twentieth-century design mindset. At one point, with the advent of commercially available nuclear electrical power sources, the promise of electrical power "too cheap to meter" (Adams 2005) led to greater reliance on even larger and more complex heating, ventilating, and air conditioning systems to offset any comfort problems created by thermal deficiencies in the building. This expanding cycle of energy use and design insensitivity continued well into the 1970s. In the 1990s, energy-sensitive designs began to gain popularity and, with the rise of greater public demand for sustainability, have taken firm hold of the building industry.

Conversely, more recently constructed residential buildings have lower EUIs (table 3.2) than those built in the decades before them. Houses of the early twentieth century use more energy than those built in the subsequent decades. This has prompted calls to upgrade the energy performance of these older residences. The major factors at issue are the amount of insulation used, the performance of existing windows, infiltration controls, and mechanical and electrical system efficiencies.

Table 3.2

Average Energy Consumption (in kBtu/sf) for Residential Buildings

Before 1939	56
1940–1949	54
1950–1959	49
1960–1969	47
1970–1979	46
1980–1989	41
1990–1999	39
2000–2001	37

Source: US Energy Information Administration (2010).

Embodied Energy

Another performance metric is embodied energy (table 3.3), which is "the energy used to process the materials required to construct the building and that needed to put them into place" (Advisory Council on Historic Preservation [ACHP] 1979b: 6). Subsequent research has refined this definition by classifying the *initial embodied energy* as *direct energy*, used to transport building products to the site and construct the building, and *indirect energy*, used to acquire, process, and manufacture the building materials and transportation energy related to these activities. In addition, *recurring embodied energy* has been identified as the "energy consumed to maintain, repair, restore, refurbish or replace materials, components or systems during the life of the building" (CanadianArchitect.com n.d.).

In 1979, the ACHP published the report *Assessing the Energy Conservation Benefits of Historic Preservation: Methods and Examples*, which considered the energy investment originally used to create the building materials and construct a historic building. In addition to considering embodied energy, this report added *operational energy* and *demolition energy* as measurements of conservation benefits. Operational energy is simply the energy needed to operate the facility and is the result of the local climate, occupancy characteristics, and physical attributes of the building. Demolition energy is the energy

Table 3.3

Embodied Energy of Common Construction Materials

	MJ/kg	MJ/m^3	Btu/lb	Btu/ft^3
Stone	0.79	2,030	340	54,485
Concrete	1.3	3,180	559	85,351
Lumber	2.5	1,380	1,075	37,039
Brick	2.5	5,170	1,075	138,763
Aluminum (recycled)	8.1	21,870	3,483	586,991
Steel (recycled)	8.9	37,210	3,827	998,716
Glass	15.9	37,550	6,837	1,007,842
Steel	32	251,200	13,760	6,742,208
Plastic (polyvinyl chloride)	70	93,620	30,100	2,512,761
Aluminum	227	515,700	97,610	13,841,388

Source: CanadianArchitect.com (n.d.). Conversion from metric to the inch–pound system by author.

needed to raze, load, and haul away demolition materials but does not include any energy savings from recycled or salvaged materials (ACHP 1979a: 8).

The National Trust for Historic Preservation (NTHP) was an early advocate promoting the inherent energy savings accrued by reusing buildings rather than replacing them with entirely new buildings. But the attitudes of the era did not foster broad acceptance of the concept. Even today the argument for measuring embodied energy to justify the retention of a building is met with skepticism. In business accounting terms, embodied energy represents a sunk cost, which, except as a baseline for potential recurring savings accrued when compared with an alternative solution, is not included in decisions about future expenses. Although the arguments for avoiding the energy consumed in demolition and the embodied energy used to create a new building remain viable, what has emerged in the past two decades is the concept of avoided impacts, or minimizing (if not eliminating) energy use for demolition and new construction. The avoided impacts have been expressed in a number of ways in a broad spectrum of business decisions. An early example of this was the Environmental Protection Agency "Green Lights" program, which advocated the use of energy-efficient lighting both as a money-saving strategy and as a means to reduce energy consumption that in turn reduced the impact of power plant emissions and improve air quality. Expansion of the conceptual framework for embodied energy has occurred in other sectors to include embodied carbon and embodied water (Carroon 2010: 260–161). Quantification methods that incorporate embodied carbon (e.g., inventory of carbon and energy, the embodied carbon metric, and the carbon footprint calculator) and embodied water (e.g., water footprint) are gaining in usage as well.

This perspective also necessitates understanding that any energy used to create and construct a new building must be recovered before that new building saves any energy that contributes toward sustainability goals. A new "sustainable" house may take 12–15 years to recover the energy used to create and transport the building materials to the job site and fabricate the building. Razing a house to replace it with a similar but more energy-efficient house (which some call conspicuous conservation) (Curtis 2008) will nearly double the recovery period because of the demolition and transport energy and the embodied energy of the original house.

When many sustainability proponents talk of creating a sustainable environment by focusing solely on tearing down old buildings and replacing them with buildings that are more energy efficient, they typically justify the benefits based solely on the lower operational energy usage of the new building compared with the existing building. This view does not account for the embodied energy needed to construct the new building nor the demolition energy needed to remove the existing building, and it disregards the embodied energy in the existing building. As Mike Jackson of the Illinois State Historic Preservation Office (SHPO) states,

> Embodied energy deserves to be another factor in the equation of sustainable design, particularly for historic preservation. The built environment represents a huge resource that can be conserved and made efficient for the twenty-first century challenge of fossil fuel exhaustion. . . . By combining preservation principles and the concept of embodied energy, a stronger argument for the environmental benefits of building reuse can be made. (Jackson 2005: 51)

In support of this statement, Jackson provided the following two cases, which illustrate how the inclusion of embodied energy, demolition energy, and differences in energy consumption projections between new and existing buildings can be interpreted, even when the new building is constructed to high-performance building standards.

CASE I
Do nothing to the existing building and build a new building. The existing building will be reused by a different user.

Embodied energy for new building: 1,200 kBtu/sf
Existing building annual operating energy: 70 kBtu/sf
New building annual operating energy: 35 kBtu/sf

Calculate the energy recovery rate (the consumption difference between the new and the existing buildings):

Energy recovery rate = Energy rate$_{existing}$ – Energy rate$_{new}$ = 70 – 35 = 35 kBtu/sf.

Calculate the recovery period for the embodied energy expended to construct the new building:

Energy recovery period = Initial embodied energy/Energy recovery rate = 1,200/35 = 34.2 years.

It will take 34.2 years to recover the energy used to construct the building before any energy is saved.

CASE 2

Salvage a portion of the existing building and demolish the remainder. Replace it with a new building.

Lost embodied energy for existing building: 1,200 kBtu/sf
Recovered embodied energy for salvaged materials: −400 kBtu/sf
Embodied energy for new building: 1,200 kBtu/sf
Total embodied energy of the project: 2,000 kBtu/sf
Existing building annual operating energy: 70 kBtu/sf
New building annual operating energy: 35 kBtu/sf

Calculate the energy recovery rate:

Energy recovery rate = Energy rate$_{existing}$ − Energy rate$_{new}$ = 70 − 35 = 35 kBtu/sf.

Calculate the period needed to recover the embodied energy expended to construct the new building:

Energy recovery period = Initial embodied energy/Energy recovery rate = 2,000/35 = 57.2 years.

It will take 57.2 years to recover the energy used to construct the new building and demolish or salvage the existing building before any real energy is saved.

Note that without the embodied energy from salvage, this period increases to 68.6 years. Salvage and deconstruction currently represent a small fraction of what their embodied energy savings could be when they are fully available nationwide.

Case 1 shows that the recovery period is excessive even if the owner simply opted to build on open suburban land. This approach contributes to green sprawl, as described in chapter 1. Case 2 presents a controversial point that many designers and property owners do not understand: the significance of the demolished building's lost embodied energy. In each scenario, the energy recovery period exceeds the expected useful lives of many buildings being constructed today. There is no real return on investment in terms of energy because following the mindset of "demolish and rebuild" or "build new in the suburban periphery" would repeat these wasteful practices before the recovery period concludes.

Material Flow

"Reduce, reuse, and recycle" (3R) is the mantra to keep recyclable materials in use and out of landfills. As noted in *Green Builders* (NJN Public Television and Radio 2009), building construction consumes 40 percent of world's resources and contributes 40 percent of the material going into landfills. This flow could be reduced by reusing buildings, which has been called the "highest" (Young 1998), "most efficient" (Cockram 2005: B.1.2), and "ultimate" (Rypkema 2007a; Young 2008b) form of recycling. The 3R philosophy has public support when it comes to aluminum, glass, and plastic containers but falls short of the same public application when it comes to buildings. Donovan Rypkema (2007b) noted that a typical building in an American downtown is perhaps 25 feet wide and 120 feet deep (fig. 3.1), and to tear it down would wipe out the entire environmental benefit from 1,344,000 aluminum cans that were recycled—just in terms of the comparative volume of material sent to a landfill. This does not include the embodied energy lost.

One alternative to razing a building is to move the building in its entirety. Wood-framed buildings have been routinely moved despite the potential obstructions posed by overhead telephone and power lines. Moving masonry buildings is more problematic. The sheer volume and weight of masonry buildings, especially when coupled with the perceived challenge of adequately stabilizing unreinforced masonry construction, have often precluded their being moved out of the path of the developer's wrecking ball. Two recent examples show how the concept of recycling and resource reuse can be accomplished in spectacular but increasingly attainable fashion.

These include the relocation of the Odd Fellows Hall (OFH) in Salt Lake City, Utah and the Showley Brothers Candy Factory in San Diego, California.

Figure 3.1. The landfill impact of the demolition of one typical 25- × 120-foot commercial building (example shown on the left is from Bryan, Texas) is equivalent in volume to 1,334,000 aluminum cans. This comparison does not take into account the embodied energy lost in the demolition.

In Salt Lake City, the plan for a proposed addition to the Frank Moss US Federal Courthouse required demolition of the 1891 OFH that was listed on the National Register of Historic Places (NRHP). The OFH, constructed primarily of unreinforced masonry, was located on an adjoining parcel on the same block as the courthouse and was estimated to weigh 6 million pounds. The Utah Heritage Foundation owned a façade easement on the building and opposed the demolition. After several years of negotiation, the General Services Administration, which is required by regulation to safeguard NRHP resources, agreed to move the building to a site across the street (fig. 3.2). The building was successfully relocated, and the General Services Administration is seeking a buyer for it.

In San Diego, redevelopment plans in the area of PETCO Park targeted the demolition of a three-story, 30,000-square-foot, unreinforced masonry building: the Showley Brothers Candy Company Building, built in 1924. However, instead of demolition, the building was moved across the street and out of harm's way. One analyst later estimated that preserving the building's 3 million pounds of brick saved the embodied energy equivalent of powering 145 homes for a year. The owners are investigating using the property for a

Figure 3.2. The Odd Fellows Hall in Salt Lake City, Utah was saved from demolition by moving it across the street.

restaurant and commercial office space (Save Our Heritage Organisation 2011; Sandiegotraveltips.com 2011).

In many cities, deconstruction and salvage companies remove materials from the construction and demolition (C&D) waste stream. The C&D waste stream is composed of bricks, concrete, masonry, soil, lumber, paving materials, shingles, glass, plastics, aluminum, steel, drywall, insulation, roofing materials, plumbing fixtures, electrical materials, siding, packaging, and tree stumps. These operations provide resources used by many preservationists to obtain duplicate components for preservation or adaptive use projects. Although deconstructing and recycling building materials is an increasingly important part of building demolition, the full potential impact of this activity has yet to be reached because the infrastructure for its broader implementation is still in development. The Institute for Local Self-Reliance (ILSR) reports,

> The EPA estimates that in 2003, an estimated 170 million tons of debris were generated from building, renovation and demolition projects across the United States. Through deconstruction and recovery, much of this material can be diverted from landfills and reused. (ILSR n.d.)

Although the potential for reusing salvaged and deconstructed materials in their existing form occurs primarily in the preservation and renovation sector, this represents a small percentage of the market, and the remainder is typically ground up, shredded, or reduced to its components and combined with raw materials to make products with "recycled content." Given the practice of disposing C&D wastes in a landfill, communities, states, and federal agencies have instituted standards and ordinances to reshape these market forces. ILSR further states,

> Communities can encourage the recycling of materials by making recovery part of the permitting process. A number of communities have passed local ordinances requiring recovery of C&D materials. In 1996, Portland, Oregon passed an ordinance requiring job-site recycling on all construction projects with a value exceeding $25,000. In 1999, Atherton, California passed an ordinance that requires all construction, renovation and demolition projects to divert fifty percent of waste from landfills. Within the city, all buildings slated for demolition are made available for deconstruction. The city of Chicago has a mandatory 50 percent recycling rate for C&D as of 2007. (ILSR n.d.)

If the retention of an existing building is not possible, then, with sufficient awareness of the benefits of deconstruction, the demand for these services will grow and become a universal part of construction activity (fig. 3.3).

An analysis conducted on the G. H. Schettler House renovation in Salt Lake City, Utah compared material flows of three alternative cases commonly found in current design and construction practice (Young 2004b). The house is a two-story, detached single-family brick house (fig. 3.4) constructed in 1904 and located in a local and national historic district. In 2000, the house was updated to meet the demands of twenty-first-century urban living. All the mechanical, electrical, and plumbing systems were replaced to increase the livability of the building. Other improvements included weatherizing windows and doors, adding attic insulation, replacing the roof, upgrading bedroom windows to meet fire and life safety codes, and installing high-efficiency appliances, low-flow plumbing fixtures, and programmable controls for the heating, ventilation, and air conditioning (HVAC) system and exterior lighting. The project, which can be described as a gut remodel, also replaced all the deteriorated plaster on the interior walls and restored or upgraded all interior finishes. Altogether, the upgrades resulted in a 37 percent reduction in heating loads and a 22 percent reduction in cooling loads. The project was a Utah Residential Tax Credit project that came under both local Historic Landmark Commission and SHPO/National Park Service review for adherence to local design guidelines and the *Secretary of the Interior's Standards*.

The goal of the research was to compare the aggregated flow of new materials going to the house and demolition materials leaving the house for the landfill. For the comparison, the analysis defined three cases. Case 1 is the retention and rehabilitation of the existing house in keeping with the primary tenets of stewardship of the built environment. Case 2 is the construction of a similar house in the suburbs, representing the favored approach for many people today. Case 3 is the demolition and replication of the existing house to represent a conservative estimate of the material flows of the "monster home" invasions occurring in older neighborhoods nationwide. In this case, the conservative estimate is based on the fact that the replacement house is the same square footage as the original house, whereas in practice the replacement is typically a much larger "monster home."

By calculating the amount of new materials used in the construction and the potential C&D waste stream of each scenario, the study analyzes the material flows, including the extraction of new raw materials and the impacts that

a

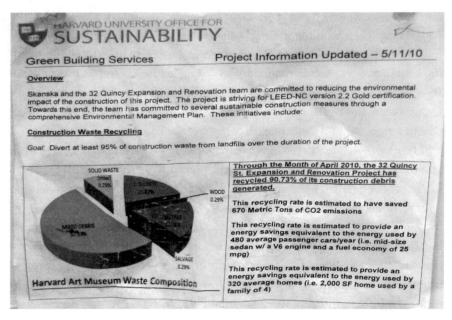

b

Figure 3.3. (a) The 32 Quincy Street (Harvard Art Museum) expansion and renovation is an example how construction and demolition waste streams can be diverted from the landfill. (b) A notice posted in the public viewing area notes, "Through the month of April 2010, the [project] has recycled 90.73% of its construction debris generated." The percentages by material type are mixed debris, 52.33 percent; concrete, 20.52 percent; metal, 17.28 percent; solid waste, 9.28 percent; wood, 0.29 percent; and salvage, 0.29 percent.

Figure 3.4. G. H. Schettler House, Salt Lake City, Utah.

the construction and demolition wastes could have on the landfill (box 3.2). Using Case 1 as a baseline, the analysis revealed that both of the other two cases generated significantly more material flows, respectively 4 times and 7.4 times as much as Case 1. In this framework, the analysis clearly demonstrated that Case 1, the retention and rehabilitation of the existing house, had the lowest overall aggregate of material flowing to and from the house.

Life Cycle Analysis

The previous two topics illustrated the potential analytical tools available in their broadest terms of embodied energy and material flows. However, as sustainability parameters have become more refined, a method defining the overall impacts on the environment was deemed a vital part of the analysis. That method is now known as life cycle analysis (LCA). According to Wayne B. Trusty, president of the Athena Sustainable Materials Institute (ASMI), which specializes in LCA studies, LCA is used for assessing the environmental performance of a product over its full life cycle. Also commonly described as cradle-to-grave or cradle-to-cradle analysis, environmental performance is measured in terms of such potential avoided impacts as

Box 3.2

Material Flow Analysis for G. H. Schettler House

Case 1: Rehabilitate Original House

New materials needed:	24.5 tons
Construction waste:	22.8 tons
Total material stream:	47.3 tons

85.9% recycled content from original construction.

Case 2: Build New House in the Suburbs

New materials needed:	173.5 tons
Construction waste:	8.9 tons
Total material stream:	182.4 tons,

$\approx 4 \times$ Case 1

0% recycled content (no original construction to reuse).

Case 3: Demolish House and Rebuild Comparable New House (but not a monster home)

New materials needed:	173.5 tons
Construction waste:	178.3 tons
Total material stream:	351.8 tons,

$\approx 7.4 \times$ Case 1

0% or only nominal recycled content from original construction.

- Fossil fuel depletion
- Other nonrenewable resource use
- Water use
- Global warming potential
- Stratospheric ozone depletion
- Ground-level ozone (smog) creation
- Nutrification or eutrophication of water bodies
- Acidification and acid deposition (dry and wet)
- Toxic releases to air, water, and land

These are indicators of environmental loadings that can result from the manufacture, use, and disposal of a product (Trusty 2003: 2). The values for these parameters are part of a complex software modeling system that has more affinity for new construction because the current associative data are more readily available. As described by Jean Carroon, principal at Goody Clancy and author of *Sustainable Preservation: Greening Existing Buildings*, LCA is the holy grail of environmental evaluation. The National Renewable Energy Laboratory maintains a publicly available database known as the US Life Cycle Inventory. The ASMI assists in maintaining the database and provides two analytical tools for LCA assessment of whole buildings and assemblies: the Athena Impact Estimator and the EcoCalculator, developed in collaboration with the University of Minnesota and Morrison Hirschfield Consulting Engineers. The Green Building Initiative commissioned the EcoCalculator for use with its Green Globes assessment and rating system (Carroon 2010: 260).

Applying LCA to an entire building rather than a product presents problems resulting from the high number of variables to consider (Tyler, Ligibel, and Tyler 2009: 304). Despite this difficulty, a study performed on four historic buildings in Canada revealed that in each case, the retention of the existing building had more favorable values than its removal and replacement with new construction. One particular finding that supports reuse was that the projected energy use in the "best renovated building" models for the reused building was equivalent to or better than the projections for the "best new building" models for a replacement building (ASMI 2009).

The use of the EcoCalculator has not been limited to projects in Canada. The Epstein Group used the EcoCalculator to determine the environmental impacts of reusing the 1946 office building that currently serves as their main office in Atlanta. This reuse project, located in the Martin Luther King Historic District, demonstrates the owner's commitment to sustainability. The building was dilapidated in 2009 when the owner decided to renovate and expand it. The Athena EcoCalculator helped the team understand the environmental impacts of design decisions and assess options for retaining or replacing several existing building components (e.g., the roof deck and joists, the second floor assembly, and exterior walls). The building earned LEED-NC Platinum certification and is considered one of the greenest buildings in Georgia (ASMI 2011). This project shows how LEED has become more attuned to reusing buildings than the prior versions.

Preservation Green Lab (2012: ix) significantly expanded the evidence for supporting the LCA approach when it released its findings for a broader spectrum of common reuse scenarios. The scenarios include reusing commercial buildings, mixed-use buildings, elementary schools, and single-family and multifamily residential buildings and converting a warehouse to an office or residential building. The findings demonstrate that, with the exception of converting a warehouse to a residence,

> It takes between 10 to 80 years for a new building that is 30 percent more efficient than an average performing existing building to overcome, through efficient operations, the negative climate change impacts related to the construction process.

The potential advantages for the conversion from warehouse to residential begin to decline as substantial amounts of new construction materials are added to the building as part of the conversion. This suggests that greater care must be taken when selecting materials that will maximize environmental savings and improve energy performance.

Architectural Form as Environmental Control

Early vernacular buildings worldwide were constructed using methods and designs that had been tuned through time to meet the demands of local climates. Long before, and even in the modern era, vernacular builders understood the opportunities that passive heating, cooling, and lighting systems presented. This understanding manifests itself in the use of architectural form as environmental control (fig. 3.5).

Historic buildings in several eras were designed with many features that responded to climate and site (fig. 3.6). When appropriately restored and reused, these features can reinvigorate the sustainable aspects of the building. Today's sustainable building technology can supplement these original climatic adaptations without compromising historic character (WBDG 2010b).

Placement of doors and windows, shading devices, thermal mass (e.g., stone, brick, adobe), and daylighting all increase thermal and visual comfort without mechanical systems and modern electric lighting. As vernacular

Figure 3.5. The cliff dwellings (reconstructed) at Mesa Verde National Park illustrate the aspects of vernacular architecture that stand the test of time. Incorporating such features as orientation for passive sun control, local materials, thermal mass, and natural ventilation, the buildings provided protection from the harsh climate of the American Southwest.

traditions developed in response to local climate demands, this awareness provided insights into building orientation, size, massing, ceiling height, and proximity to other buildings. As the profession of architecture emerged, architectural training included these aspects as inherent good design practice. Roman architect Vitruvius described the aspects of good design as firmness, commodity (usefulness), and delight. Through the millennia, buildings have been designed and constructed using these principles. By the industrial revolution, these low-technology principles were enhanced by the introduction of fundamental mechanical heating and cooling systems.

Today, two of the primary vernacular strategies, passive thermal design and daylighting, are being rediscovered and used in new buildings but can still be found on many historic and existing buildings built well before modern HVAC and lighting systems came into use.

Figure 3.6. This house in Natchitoches, Louisiana incorporates numerous features that improve its passive thermal performance, including overhangs (used as porches) to protect from summer sun, louvered shutters for light and wind control, and light surface colors to reduce solar gain.

Passive Thermal Design

Passive thermal design relies on the building to mitigate the effects of the local climate. In the broadest terms, these principles include form and volume, orientation, sun and wind control devices, and the use of thermal mass.

Compact forms were used in cold climates to limit the surface area exposed to cold temperatures (fig. 3.7). Buildings were also built in small clusters or with attached party walls to reduce heat loss. Larger forms and volumes were preferred in hot, humid climates. High ceilings (12–24 feet) allowed warm air to rise out of the occupied zone (fig. 3.8). In smaller houses, shade and cross-ventilation provided relief from the heat.

Orientation relative to the sun's path was a consideration that played into how a building was located on a site. The daily movement of the sun across the sky provides the greatest solar control along the south façade. As a consequence, the longest side of a building was oriented to face south or slightly east of south. When counterposed with the direction for cold northerly winter

Figure 3.7. Buildings in cold climates are more compact, have fewer windows, and are oriented for solar access. Shown here is a small house in Essex, New York.

windows, this created a sheltered area at the front of the building (fig. 3.9). Sun along the western side is more difficult to control, and buildings with their long façade facing west have greater overheating problems in summer months if there is no planned shading to help control exposure to sunlight.

Porches and balconies were used as a sun control or shading device and as social or utility spaces (fig. 3.10). Overhangs created by the porch roof and decking provide shelter on the façade of the building at and below the porch. Porches were used for socializing with passersby and guests as well as utilitarian uses such as preparing meals, doing laundry, and sleeping. The porch emerged as a social phenomenon in the nineteenth century but had migrated to the rear of the house in the form of a deck or patio by the mid-twentieth century. In colder, northern climates, porches were not as popular early on because they obstructed the solar access needed for passive solar warming in winter. The emergence of new urbanism at the end of the twentieth century led to the rediscovery of the front porch as a social phenomenon where the cultivation of social capital occurs (Sander 2002: 213–234); consequently, porches are a common feature in new urbanist projects.

a

b

Figure 3.8. Large building volumes, high ceilings, and cross-ventilation can increase comfort in humid regions. Shown here are **(a)** the San Francisco Plantation in Garyville, Louisiana and **(b)** the dining room at Oatlands Plantation in Natchitoches, Louisiana. (© R. A. Young; interior image used with permission from the National Park Service.)

Figure 3.9. Orientation plays an important role in sun exposure. Typically buildings with their longer orientation running east to west have better passive solar performance than buildings with the longer orientation running north to south because the admission of direct sunlight can be more readily controlled with horizontal shading elements.

Figure 3.10. Porches, balconies, and landscaping can control sun and create shade.

Where porches and balconies were not an option, shutters could be used to control sunlight and air flow (fig. 3.11). In temperate and humid areas, the shutters were louvered, whereas in cold climates the shutters could be a solid panel to block cold winter winds. Projecting shading devices, fixed canopies, and recessed windows were used to control sunlight (fig. 3.12). Operable windows were used to control the ventilation from outside air. In smaller vernacular buildings in cold climates, windows were smaller and fewer in number.

In other instances, when porches or fixed canopies were not an option, operable shading devices could be used to control sun exposure (fig. 3.13). The awning could be retracted when not needed or fully extended during periods of hot or inclement weather.

Arcades along the perimeter of a building or flanking an interior courtyard provided relief from direct sunlight. Openings such as doors and arches along the perimeter permitted cross-ventilation. In drier climates, fountains and pools provided evaporative cooling. In more humid environments, a fountain

Figure 3.11. Shutters provide control for sunlight and ventilation. Shown here are shutters on a house in Galveston, Texas. Windows in warmer climates are typically larger to provide greater opportunity for summer ventilation.

a

Figure 3.12. Sculptural form or even simple projecting shading devices were used to control sunlight. Windows could also be recessed to provide partial shading. Shown here are (a) the Crescent Hotel and (b) the Carlyle Hotel in Miami, Florida.

b

a

b

Figure 3.13. Awnings were used for sunlight control and shade. Shown here are (a) the Beaumont Hotel in Ouray, Colorado and (b) The Hotel of South Beach in Miami, Florida.

contributes to increased humidity or dampness and is used primarily as ornament or for other needs.

As air warms and becomes more buoyant, it rises by natural convection. The resulting stack effect can be relieved by operable skylights or openings at the top of a space (fig. 3.14). In historic and other older buildings this can be seen through the use of towers, atria, and belvederes as a precursor to the modern solar chimney. Similarly, openings on the windward and leeward sides of the building can increase comfort by creating cross-ventilation through both horizontal and vertical spaces. This phenomenon is the basis for the study of computational fluid dynamics. This process occurs naturally or can be emulated by mechanical systems with an attendant direct cost of energy to operate fans. When cooler overnight conditions permit extraction of the absorbed heat, this forms the basis of free convective cooling, which is now called night flush cooling.

Within a single space, transoms in combination with double-hung windows took advantage of the stack effect and cross-ventilation (fig. 3.15). With

Figure 3.14. The Pension Building, completed in 1887 in Washington, DC, shows how the stack effect and cross-ventilation were integrated into commercial buildings. (Photo: © R. A. Young, shown here with permission of the National Building Museum.)

the transom and the upper sash and lower sash open, cross ventilation releases warm air otherwise trapped at the ceiling. Combined with an adjoining atrium or stairwell, this can also be used to create the convective cooling process described earlier. However, contemporary fire and life safety codes often prohibit the operable transom in nonresidential buildings to control smoke migration into rooms adjoining the source of the smoke. The reintegration of these time-proven, natural ventilation concepts has been hailed as innovative in today's design thinking and has been lauded as a significant aspect of sustainable design.

Since the early twentieth century, there has been a shift away from thermal mass in the exterior building envelope (fig. 3.16). Masonry (adobe, brick, concrete, and stone) is more important as thermal mass than as an insulator. Many performance indices that rely simply on thermal resistance (R-value) of a material neglect the fact that masonry acts as a heat sink that absorbs heat and slows the exchange of heat for a longer period of time when compared with a less thermally massive material such as aluminum, and this can have important

Figure 3.15. (a) Double-hung windows and (b) a transom provide opportunities for ventilation and nighttime cooling. The top sash is lowered at night, and the transom is opened to create an air flow path that relieves heat buildup at the ceiling.

Figure 3.16. In the early twentieth century, the use of masonry (thermal mass) gave way to a greater use of curtain walls composed of aluminum or glass. Shown here in the foreground is the Clift Building in Salt Lake City, Utah, completed in 1920, and in the background is the Wells Fargo Center (originally the American Stores Building), completed in 1998.

energy conservation implications. In some cases, this thermal shift may take several hours and may help meet nighttime heating needs or be reradiated to the night sky directly or through convective flow, using natural or mechanical ventilation methods. This lack of understanding of how the R-value of masonry is tempered by the thermal flywheel effect has led to many misunderstandings about its energy performance. Conversely, materials such as aluminum, glass, and plastics may transmit heat very quickly by comparison.

The introduction of steel and reinforced concrete structural framing systems near the end of the nineteenth century led to the development of curtain walls, which are a non-load-bearing enclosure system that does not support the roof. Curtain walls and structural frames eventually replaced the widespread use of masonry load-bearing construction by the mid-twentieth century (fig. 3.17). As curtain wall technology progressed, buildings were tightly sealed to

Figure 3.17. The shift away from thermal mass occurred throughout the twentieth century. The Commonwealth Building (originally the Equitable Building) in Portland, Oregon (1948) was the first fully curtain wall enclosed building.

enable HVAC systems to control thermal comfort. As air conditioning became more widespread, the acceptable range for thermal comfort narrowed. In the process, the use of operable windows in commercial buildings largely disappeared. As office buildings were built in the mid-twentieth century, HVAC comfort control began to dominate. Subsequently, architecture of the period became disconnected from local climatic forces, and many of the inherent design principles well known in the early twentieth century eventually fell out of use (fig. 3.18).

Additionally, curtain walls (and aluminum and vinyl siding on residential buildings) were often installed on existing commercial buildings simply to modernize the appearance and reduce maintenance or operation costs, and often destroyed historic character-defining features during installation (fig. 3.19).

Figure 3.18. As curtain wall technology evolved, the use of operable windows gave way to HVAC control. The only fresh air came in through the mechanical system.

Figure 3.19. Installation methods for curtain walls can damage or remove the character-defining features of the original construction and compromise the historic integrity of the buildings. Shown here is damage caused by a curtain wall installation that has since been removed.

Daylighting

An important character-defining feature of many pre–World War II buildings is the use of daylighting. Increased daylighting and reduced reliance on
electric lighting is a unifying goal of contemporary high-performance building standards. Many passive thermal concepts have an overlapping benefit for
controlling daylight. However, daylight is not necessarily synonymous with
sunlight. Although sunlight penetration does provide illumination, it also introduces heat gain. In cold climates this may be desirable, but in warmer climates it contributes to the cooling load and can cause thermal discomfort. The
modern use of daylighting was led by Alvar Aalto for projects he designed in
overcast areas adjoining the North Sea.

As technology evolved at the turn of the twentieth century to facilitate construction of taller buildings, it became evident that the use of atria in buildings
with daylighting and ventilation accommodations provided access to natural
light (fig. 3.20), which is another goal of contemporary high-performance
building standards. Ceiling height played a factor in building design because
as a rule the useful penetration of daylight extends to 2.5 times the height of the
top of the window into the space. Consideration of these two factors yields a
commercial building that typically has double-loaded corridors extending outward from a central service core. These buildings have been called alphabet
buildings because their floor plates resemble block forms of the letters E, H, I,
L, O, T, and U, or combinations thereof.

In small commercial buildings, the storefront consisted of display windows flanking a recessed doorway, which were together topped by transoms
or clerestory windows. Using the 2.5 multiplier meant that a combination of
windows whose tops were 12 feet high would yield a useful daylighting depth
of 30 feet into the building interior. When ceiling height and building width
did not permit useful daylight to sufficiently penetrate the space interior in
low-rise buildings, rooftop monitors, clerestories, and skylights were used, especially in industrial manufacturing or sales facilities where floor space was at
a premium (fig. 3.21).

Many older buildings being rehabilitated today are industrial, light manufacturing, and warehouse buildings, which historically had larger, open spaces
within them. The openness of these spaces conforms well to large open office
plans. Because the open space is a character-defining feature, installation of

Figure 3.20. Early twentieth-century skyscrapers, such as the Chicago Board of Trade Building, constructed in 1930, used irregular floor plates to maximize opportunities for daylight and ventilation access.

office space is readily accomplished. Conversely, the spaces and historic character-defining features found in double-loaded corridors of alphabet buildings typically cannot be combined into a single space without jeopardizing tax credits because removing these walls destroys the historic integrity. Rather than create large open floor plans, building owners can create spaces that target smaller business operations that seek smaller spaces or can lease an entire floor.

The introduction of the fluorescent lamp in 1937 changed how buildings were designed. The irregular floor plates gave way to rectangular floor plates lit by continuous rows of fluorescent lighting (with lighting densities approaching 5 watts/sf). Daylighting gave way to electric lighting, which eliminated the need for higher ceilings. With the rectangular floor plates, lowered ceilings, and cheap electricity to power them, fluorescent lighting became the norm. To address brightness problems, visible light transmission in glazing products

a

b

c

was significantly reduced by adding tinting or reflective coatings. As window glazing strategies changed, modern design became further climatically disconnected as shading devices on the exterior were eliminated and the need to reduce solar heat gains through the glass became imperative. The occupants' need for visual and thermal comfort led to even greater dependence on electric lighting and HVAC systems. It was during this era that Americans began to expect uniformly constant temperatures at home, at the office, and elsewhere.

The recognition of the need to change these practices began with the 1970s energy crises and has continued growing since then. Today's digital world invites the use of electronic control devices such as occupancy sensors, programmable thermostats, and even digital control from remote locations. With the advent of electronic ballasts in the late twentieth century, the opportunity for dimming fluorescent lighting in response to available daylight came to fruition. There are additional benefits to reusing buildings that were designed according to traditional daylighting principles. Subsequent studies have revealed that access to daylight improves productivity in office spaces and increases retail sales. Workers with access to daylight in their workspace report better health, and students score better on standardized tests (Heschong Mahone Group 2011).

Increasing Sustainability

Sustainable design is most often measured by how a building is sited or a community is designed to mitigate sprawl and its attendant environmental degradation. As discussed, many older buildings already have characteristics that are highly valued in contemporary design for their contributions to sustainability (fig. 3.22). Particularly true of buildings built before the rise of the midcentury modern buildings, these design aspects are being rediscovered by a number of architects who are now using them on new construction and rehabilitating

Figure 3.21. Three methods for naturally lighting interior spaces: (a) The Ford Motor Company Building in Salt Lake City, Utah used roof monitors (at right in the image); (b) the Utah State Capitol used a vaulted skylight; and (c) these 1890s retail buildings in Mt. Pleasant, Utah (right) used display windows and transoms.

Figure 3.22. Although the practice of reusing buildings is timeless, retrofitting existing historic buildings to increase sustainability has been ongoing for the past three decades. Shown here are **(a)** the Audubon House (completed in 1891, retrofit in 1993) and **(b)** the Empire State Building (completed in 1931, ongoing retrofit, expected tenant space modification completion in 2013). The Audubon House retrofit was completed well before the high-performance standards in use today (Croxton Collaborative 1994). The Empire State Building achieved LEED-EB Gold certification and is being celebrated as an iconic way to update historic buildings (Bose 2010: 27).

a

b

them on reuse projects. Two notable examples of this are the Christman Construction Headquarters in Lansing, Michigan, which earned the world's first LEED Triple Platinum status, and the Big D Construction Headquarters in Salt Lake City, Utah, which earned the first LEED Gold status in Utah.

The two primary areas targeted for sustainability upgrades are the building envelope and the mechanical, electrical, and plumbing (MEP) systems' energy use optimization. At any building scale, there is lively debate about the extent to which envelope modifications (fig. 3.23) compromise authenticity and historic integrity and whether they should be compromised at all.

Building Envelope

Performance of the building envelope (i.e., windows, doors, walls, ceilings, roofs, and floors) can be improved through weatherization and increasing or controlling the admission of natural light. The first concern for many building owners is the efficiency of their windows and how to upgrade them. Inappropriate replacements (fig. 3.24) have led to much debate between property owners, neighbors, and preservationists. Although there are incentives for energy upgrades through such programs as the American Reinvestment and Recovery Act (Recovery Act), this federally backed program triggers a design review when applied to buildings on or eligible for the NRHP.

Much has been said about the energy savings from replacement windows in a retrofit of an existing building. What often goes unsaid or is misunderstood is that, because heated air naturally rises, the amount of conductive energy lost through windows is lower than heat lost through infiltration and heat rising into underinsulated attics and roofs. Many building scientists and energy auditors understand this and recommend making rooms less drafty by installing storm windows and weatherstripping, recaulking around openings in the building envelope, and sealing openings leading to or from unheated spaces (e.g., attics, basements, stairwells, mechanical rooms).

Although window manufacturers extol the virtues of their vinyl-based products, one-for-one replacement of wood windows with more efficient units is not cost-effective in terms of simple payback (box 3.3). A study prepared for the Collingswood Historic District Commission (Lord 2007: 43) showed that the most cost-effective solution was to add a storm window to an existing single-pane window unit (table 3.4). Similar studies demonstrate even longer payback periods for full replacement.

Figure 3.23. **(a)** The Lever House upgrade replaced the curtain wall system with a **(b)** visually comparable but higher-efficiency assembly. Conversely, in the residential sector, the approach of the deep energy retrofit includes increasing the envelope thickness by several inches for additional insulation. Both approaches raise questions about retaining historic integrity and would nullify any preservation-based funding eligibility.

a

b

a

b

Figure 3.24. These windows have been criticized for their insensitive replacement of original windows. Criticism includes **(a)** loss of historic character-defining features (reflectivity, shadow profiles) and **(b)** size mismatch.

Box 3.3

Simple Payback Analysis

Simple payback analysis is used to quickly determine how long it will take to recover the extra cost that is typically incurred when purchasing a product that provides better energy performance. Simple payback is calculated as follows:

Payback (yr) = Incremental additional cost ($)/Annual energy savings ($/yr).

For example, if you are comparing two air conditioners and the more expensive one costs an additional $100 but will save $40/year, then the payback is 100/40 = 2.5 years. Most guidelines will accept payback periods of 3 or 4 years or less, so this payback is acceptable.

For more complex upgrades using multiple products of varying useful lives, it is necessary to do a life cycle cost analysis or an internal rate of return analysis, which accounts for changes in the value of money over time and multiple equipment replacements.

Table 3.4

Payback Analysis for Window Upgrade Options

Options	Cost ($)	R-Value	Annual Btus Saved	Annual Cost Savings ($)	Payback Period (yr)
Original window (OW)	—	0.9	0	0	0
OW + Storm window	$50	2.0	722,218	13.20	3.8
Double pane	$450	1.7	625,922	11.07	40.5
Low-e double pane	$550	2.9	902,722	16.10	34.0
Low-e double pane for OW + Storm window	$550	2.9	132,407	2.29	240.0

Source: Lord (2007: 43).

The addition of a storm window realizes a payback period of 3.8 years, whereas the payback period of any other option is quite high and not economically feasible. Because the average American family moves approximately every 5 years, the original purchaser may not realize any cost savings. Recent trends also indicate that the useful life of vinyl windows is much lower than manufacturers' claims. The NTHP points out that 30 percent of vinyl replacement windows are themselves replaced within 10 years (NTHP 2009: 2). Unlike wood windows, vinyl components cannot be repaired when damaged and must be completely replaced. Despite the 15- to 20-year warranties offered by the manufacturer, manufacturers of less expensive windows, which would have a lower installed cost and shorter payback periods, may be out of business before the warranty expires. In any of the vinyl replacement window scenarios, the payback exceeds the expected life and probable availability of in-kind replacement.

Repairing wood-framed windows is cost-effective in terms of both first cost and the opportunity to replace subsequently broken or damaged parts (fig. 3.25). When muntin and sash thickness allows, glazing may also be replaced with individual lites of double-pane glass. If replacement windows are deemed absolutely necessary, consider using a *simulated divided lite* (SDL) or *true divided lite* (TDL) window. These pose advantages in that the original muntin bar profiles can be replicated on the exterior and interior faces of the window unit.

Metal sash can corrode and fail, but a more significant drawback is that, in many older types, the frames do not include a *thermal break*, and heat is constantly moving toward cooler temperatures (e.g., outward in winter, inward in summer). In this case, the best option may be to install a replacement sash that includes double-paned glazing and matches the original profile of the frame, sash, and muntins but has been manufactured to include a thermal break that cuts off the heat flow. Another alternative may be to include *laminated glass* to reduce conductive heat flow and direct solar gain.

When a building is located in a local historic district or when the project is seeking tax credits, the local historic landmarks commission and SHPO can provide guidance on window selection. Installation of inappropriate windows that do not meet the local design guidelines or the *Secretary of the Interior's Guidelines* may result in a fine and their replacement at the owner's expense or the denial of tax credits.

The second major concern for many building owners is the thermal efficiency of the building envelope. Sealing infiltration paths can reduce infiltration and heat exchange significantly. Likewise, insulating the attic will suppress the natural upward flow of heat. Insulating floors over unheated crawlspaces can keep the floor surface warmer but may have only a nominal effect on energy consumption.

The building walls are the final opportunity for insulation upgrades. The

Figure 3.25. Wood windows can often be repaired for less money than complete replacement. This helps preserve authenticity and reduces environmental concerns about the fabrication of new materials and disposal of existing ones. Shown here are (a) the before and (b) after views of a window repaired at the Moroni Opera House in Moroni, Utah by the Traditional Building Skills Institute.

a

b

insulation could be added in any of three locations: on the interior face, on the exterior face, and within the interior cavity if one exists. Each presents its own array of problems. First, adding the insulation to the interior face encroaches on the occupiable space and destroys the original surface treatments and details. Second, adding insulation to the exterior face, as is done in deep energy retrofits, destroys the exterior appearance in a similar manner as with the interior installation. Third, adding insulation to the cavity can generate numerous problems. Historically, the cavity found in masonry load-bearing walls could actually be a drainage plane situated to allow moisture penetration to drop to drainage openings below. These drainage planes should not be filled in. In all three instances, adding insulation without verifying the suitability of moisture barriers or air barriers can lead to condensation inside the wall that can cause rot, corrosion, mold, and other moisture-related problems.

In a wood-framed cavity wall or a veneer masonry wall with interior framing, cavities could be filled with blown-in or foamed-in insulation. However, filling these spaces can introduce moisture problems for the exterior cladding on the cold side of the insulation, particularly in freeze–thaw zones. In either type, the product is injected into the cavity through holes cut into the exposed surface. The propellants force the insulation into the cavity, where it follows the path of least resistance. Therefore, the obstructions caused by wiring, plumbing, fire-blocking, and other structural components can cause uneven insulation within the wall. The presence of these obstructions or the extent of coverage can be determined through nondestructive testing methods such as thermographic infrared photography before and after the installation. Many foamed-in insulations may introduce moisture in the process of installation or may create internal pressures that can dislodge interior cladding or find its way out in unexpected places (fig. 3.26). Blown-in insulations may not have integral vapor barriers, may not completely fill the cavity, or may settle (fig. 3.27)

For many historically nonsignificant buildings of the mid- and late twentieth century, weatherization may not pose any problem at all. The potential controversy arises when buildings that come under historic design review consideration are weatherized, and specific caution must be taken to avoid compromising their historic integrity. Appropriate reviewing agencies should be consulted before the modifications begin to ensure that the work will not violate preservation guidelines.

Another aspect of modifying the building envelope is to take advantage of existing daylighting elements or even to introduce new ones. As noted earlier,

Figure 3.26. Foam insulation products will seep through any gaps that they can. There are insulation foam products with expansion rates specifically formulated for use in finished cavity walls.

Figure 3.27. For residential buildings, insulating the attic floor is an effective way to reduce heat loss. This loose insulation, originally rated R38, has settled, as indicated on this installation gauge.

building envelope components such as tall windows, transoms, clerestories, and skylights along with high ceilings and atria found in older buildings provide numerous opportunities for daylighting. If not already present, these features can be added. A limiting factor is the amount of sun and brightness controls available for the glazing for buildings of the mid-twentieth-century modern movement. Ceilings in retail buildings that were previously lowered can be removed to increase daylight penetration. Interior clerestories and glass (translucent or transparent) partition walls and flooring may be added to increase daylight penetration without entirely removing the corridor walls. Multiple-floored industrial and warehouse buildings, with their existing skylights and open space, foster the creation of atria to penetrate lower floors. For example, removal of floor slabs at the Big D Construction Company Building in Salt Lake City (Young 2008c) still permitted the building to pass the *Standards* for tax credit work (fig. 3.28).

A variety of sensors, which adjust the amount of electric light according to available daylight, offer another kind of control. With the introduction of electronic ballasts in the 1990s, the combination of daylight sensors and electronic controllers can eliminate or significantly reduce electric lighting. Similarly, an occupancy sensor can activate electric lighting when people are using a space.

Mechanical, Electrical, and Plumbing Systems

In the *Standards*, MEP equipment (e.g., boilers, chillers, air-handling units) has been protected to the extent that the *Standards* recommend that original components should be retained and upgraded in place whenever possible. The broader concern relates to physical disruption and visual impact of piping and ductwork, especially on the interior finishes and spatial qualities of historically significant spaces. For buildings with significant public spaces that cannot be adapted to a raised-floor system, care must be taken to route these paths so as not to compromise the visual and physical qualities of those spaces. Concerns also include the terminal devices (e.g., air registers, radiators, lighting and plumbing fixtures) in these spaces. One specific practice that is not recommended in the *Standards* is the installation of MEP systems (e.g., mechanical equipment, solar panels, and photovoltaic panels) in locations visible from a public way. The *Standards* also recommend that this equipment and distribution networks be located in secondary spaces when possible.

a

Figure 3.28. The Big D
Construction Company
conversion of **(a)** the Fuller
Paint Company Building
in Salt Lake City, Utah
included creation of **(b)** a
three-story atrium at the
center of the building. The
project earned LEED Gold
certification and qualified
for federal historic preservation tax credits.

b

Many projects involve replacing less efficient components (e.g., burners, motors, pumps, incandescent lamps) with higher-efficiency versions. Other projects may remove, replace, or relocate portions or all of the equipment and the distribution networks. Additional strategies to improve sustainability performance and reduce costs include the following:

- Digital technology overlays
- Heat pumps
- Raised-floor air supply
- Photovoltaic panels
- Low-flow plumbing fixtures

One approach to upgrading mechanical and electrical operating systems has been through digital technology control overlays. When systems are controlled digitally, any number of control strategies can be used beyond the use of occupancy sensors and timers. Originally individual controllers were on each separate component or subsystem, but by the late twentieth century a centralized control from a remote location was available. Subsequent advances and integration with Internet communications expanded this control to remote mobile locations off-site. This technology has the ability to track usage and operational trends and tune the operating strategies to optimize energy use.

One strategy to improve the energy efficiency and indoor air quality is to enhance features that contribute to air circulation. In addition to nighttime flush cooling, which can occur as natural convection caused by the stack effect of warm air rising, it is possible to augment this air flow with mechanically powered rotary fans. Fans can be located in the higher ceiling spaces found in older buildings to direct air flow upward or downward depending on the season. Similarly, these fans can be augmented by fans operating in tandem with fresh air intake and relief air systems (fig. 3.29). In buildings with large exhaust air quantities, the energy in that air can be processed in a heat exchanger to preheat or precool incoming makeup air or domestic water service.

In addition to the nighttime flush option, the enthalpy-controlled introduction of outdoor air may be appropriate. In this situation, the heat content of the outdoor air is compared with the heat content of the conditioned air. During the cooling season, when the enthalpy of the outdoor air is less, the system shuts off the chillers and uses the less energy-intensive outdoor air directly.

a

b

Figure 3.29. (a) The rotary fan at the top of the atrium of the Big D Construction office improves the thermal qualities of the building. (b) The automated relief air louvers work with the main mechanical systems to increase nighttime flush opportunities.

For residential applications, a programmable thermostat (fig. 3.30) is the starting point for automated control. Modern digital communication controllers sourced from smart phones and minicomputers are also available to allow homeowners to control their utility systems via remote access.

Heat pumps have gained popularity in the past decade. Ground-coupled heat pumps take advantage of the thermal mass of the soil to create a heat sink–heat source relationship. Heat pumps reject heat into the soil in the summer and extract heat from the soil in the winter. This arrangement provides an efficient means of heating and cooling without significantly visually affecting the appearance of the building (fig. 3.31).

In commercial applications where there are higher ceilings, a raised-floor air supply system is a good way to provide cooling and ventilation. This system is an innovative energy saver in which distributed air rises through the occupied space rather than being blown in from above. Therefore, discharge temperatures for cooling are warmer than overhead systems and use less energy to provide the same level of comfort. Raised-floor systems also provide a versatile way to route ducts, cables, and other service systems in a concealed manner but are not a solution for every project because the raised floor may

Figure 3.30. Programmable thermostats have been proven to be an effective means to reduce energy use and costs. Payback periods of less than 1 year are common.

Figure 3.31. The Major Downey House in Salt Lake City, Utah uses an innovative heat exchange system. Although ground-coupled heat pumps are gaining widespread acceptance nationwide, the heat pump at the Major Downey House exchanges heat with the municipal sewer line adjoining the property.

conflict with existing windowsill and door heights. This approach is successful generally in industrial and warehouse reuse projects but has limited application in alphabet buildings because of the expense of installing ramps or adjusting doors and stairways.

Photovoltaics (and solar panels) have created quite a controversy in historic districts because of their appearance on primary façades or roofs viewed from a public way. When carefully located out of public view, they provide the desired power and thermal energy without visual disruption (fig. 3.32). Many retrofit projects have incorporated off-site power production (e.g., subscribing to wind energy programs offered by local utilities) to meet renewable energy use targets and have used this opportunity to meet requirements of programs such as LEED without constructing on-site equipment. The district energy strategy championed by the Preservation Green Lab noted in chapter 2 is another approach to reducing visual impact of these installations.

Water conservation is a fast-emerging sustainability concern in the twenty-

Figure 3.32. The Stratford Apartments building in Salt Lake City, Utah uses rooftop-mounted photovoltaic panels to help meet the electrical power needs of its tenants. The panels are located so that they cannot be seen from the street.

first century. Access to potable water and clean water for industrial processes is a growing problem as populations expand. For plumbing systems, a wide variety of products have been introduced to reduce flow in faucets and shower heads. Similar to lighting controls, infrared sensors in plumbing fixtures provide controls to turn water on or off and activate toilets and urinals. Numerous other plumbing products have been introduced, including low-flow or dual-flush toilets and waterless urinals. The Dana Building at the University of Michigan, built in 1903, uses a variety of alternative fixtures to reduce water consumption (McInnis and Tyler 2005). The use of localized water heaters and insulated pipes reduces the water volume (and the associated energy used to heat it) that would be wasted while waiting for water to warm up when turned on.

Water demand can be further reduced through the collection of rainwater. Many pre-twentieth-century buildings used cisterns to store rainwater; however, many of these were abandoned or removed when municipal water supplies became available. Another water reduction strategy is using graywater systems to recover water from sinks and showers for reuse in toilets and other nonculinary purposes. Some local ordinances do not allow use of these two strategies, however, so they are not appropriate for every building.

Building Codes

Building codes are created primarily with the needs of new construction in mind. Many code revisions come about in reaction to building failures, fire disasters, new technologies, and construction practices. Although the intention is to make the built environment safer and more sustainable, their adoption often creates unintended consequences. It is not unexpected, then, that the recent sustainability quantification methods, like most other industry practices, initially and primarily dealt with new construction. This approach has left proponents of preserving historic buildings and adaptively using other existing buildings to their own devices when it comes to convincing others about the viability of their efforts. These factors also have created some unintended consequences that weaken efforts toward stewardship of the built environment and the overall sustainability of a community.

As efforts to make buildings more energy efficient in the 1980s became part of the professional design community's service offerings, early standards such as ANSI/ASHRAE/IESNA Standard 90 (ASHRAE 90) were integrated into a variety of regionally based codes for new construction. Typically, the success of energy efficiency upgrades is expressed in terms of how much below the minimum ASHRAE 90 compliance level the building performance achieves. For example, a building energy consumption level that is 20 percent below the ASHRAE 90 standard uses 20 percent less than the accepted amount of energy usage for that type of building. Although this standard can be fairly benign toward existing buildings, the further reduction of energy targets may conflict with preservation projects because construction practices geared toward new construction can conflict with the intention to retain historic character-defining features.

With the introduction and adoption of the International Building Code (IBC) in 2000, regionally administered codes were discontinued. The IBC still looks primarily at new construction, which has hindered interpretation of design intentions in existing buildings. To address this oversight, the International Existing Building Code (IEBC) has been developed as a model code for communities to use in fostering a more flexible interpretation of how existing buildings can be made to perform as needed in contemporary society. Unfortunately, the IEBC has not been widely adopted or used.

In 2009, the International Codes Council announced plans to develop the International Green Construction Code (IGCC), which is a model code "focused on new and existing commercial buildings addressing green building design and performance" (International Codes Council 2011). With precedence models from smart codes that have been developed in the past decade, coupled with the efforts of organizations such as the Preservation Green Lab and its outcome-based code program, it is hoped that this code will accommodate performance goals that are friendlier to preservation and reuse projects than in the past.

In addition to using the IBC, many states and municipalities have developed high-performance building standards and smart codes. A few include existing buildings, but many look specifically at new construction. They largely leave the issues affecting reuse and preservation open for interpretation through the lens of new construction. This freedom of interpretation has not made preservation and reuse seem more attractive, however. Without direct guidelines, many developers, lenders, contractors, and designers operate only in the realm of new buildings and cannot or will not take on the "risk" of reusing a building.

Accessibility, Life Safety, and Security

Technology impacts on sustainability encompass a broad range of considerations, much broader than simple energy efficiency. These include accessibility, life safety, and security; urban heat island mitigation; and the environmental impacts of creating more sprawl versus repopulating central cities (i.e., increasing population density).

Similar to new mechanical, electrical, and plumbing system insertions, preservation of character-defining features can present a challenge when a public building is upgraded to meet Americans with Disabilities Act (ADA) compliance and life safety and security needs, which are also facets of social sustainability. In Preservation Brief 32, *Making Historic Buildings Accessible*, Jester and Park (1993) describe the various aspects of creating accessibility while respecting the historic significance of the building:

- Make the main or a prominent public entrance and primary public spaces accessible, including a path to the entrance.
- Provide access to goods, services, and programs.
- Provide accessible restroom facilities.
- Create access to amenities and secondary spaces.

As the historic significance of the building increases, so does the level of attention to sensitively inserting ADA, life safety, and security measures into the primary (public) spaces. The general approach for these enhancements (e.g., elevator upgrades, emergency egress stairs) has been to locate them in secondary spaces adjoining the primary ones, as is often done with new MEP systems as well. The *Whole Building Design Guide* has established a set of approaches to consider when incorporating new life safety and security measures into an existing building (box 3.4). Although these are intended for historically significant buildings, they can also be sensitive design considerations for rehabilitating or adaptively reusing a nonhistoric building.

In accordance with the *Standards*, the design of any of these new features should be differentiated from the historic property, and the modifications should be on scale with the historic property, visually compatible, and reversible. Reversibility is a key component of any modifications or repairs to historic buildings. Ongoing changes in technology introduce new installation methods, systems, and materials to preservation practice. The *Standards* do not recommend using any installation method, system, or material that destroys the existing character-defining features or makes it impossible to reverse the installation process and return the character-defining feature to its previous condition.

Urban Heat Islands

The built environment lends itself to forming urban heat islands where concentrations of buildings and paved surfaces collect solar energy and alter the local microclimate to be warmer and drier than surrounding suburban and rural areas. In the 1990s, the National Aeronautics and Space Administration conducted flyovers to measure the impact of the built environment on temperature. The resulting thermographic images confirmed the actual thermal impacts of heat islands, which has subsequently fostered the introduction of

Box 3.4
Whole Building Design Guide Recommendations for Accommodating Life
Safety and Security Measures in Historic Buildings

Egress: Preserve the primary, main, ceremonial entrance experience. Where existing
stairs cannot be brought into compliance without significantly changing the character
of the spaces, additional means of egress should be carefully located to preserve significant spaces while providing a minimum of two means of egress.

Fire and Smoke Separation: Design smoke separation to avoid subdividing or ob-
scuring significant spaces, such as stairways, corridors, entry areas.

Fire and Smoke Detection: Early detection of heat and smoke is critical to extin-
guishing fires with minimum damage to historic resources. Very early response/detec-
tion systems can eliminate the need for suppression systems.

Fire Suppression Systems: The purpose of fire suppression systems is to cover all
surfaces evenly. However, this can result in damage to historic finishes. Evaluate fire
loads to determine appropriate protection. Use computer modeling to identify high-
risk areas. Select and locate fire suppression systems to minimize water and subsequent mold damage to historic fabric. Alternative suppression systems such as dry
systems, mist systems, and time delay with alarms prior to activation help reduce water damage. Careful and sensitive installation of suppression systems is critical to the
preservation of the character of historic spaces.

Operational Considerations: Include operational and management solutions for
life safety and historic preservation when designing the systems. Ensure that staff and
occupants are trained to respond promptly and summon additional resources in event
of an emergency situation.

Source: WBDG (2010a).

"green" roofs on both new and existing buildings (e.g., Chicago City Hall).
These studies demonstrated that older buildings with darker roof surfaces
exposed to direct sunlight absorbed and retained heat, which elevated temperatures in the immediate local microclimate. These temperature increases
translate into higher energy costs for cooling a building. In Salt Lake City, this
phenomenon was clearly demonstrated when two downtown civic buildings
located two blocks apart had 28°F temperature difference on their roofs. The
lower temperature occurred on a building with a white roof; the hotter roof

Figure 3.33. White roofing materials can immediately reduce summer heat gains. However, it is important to understand what visual impact they will have on the building when installed.

was black. The higher temperature also fosters a higher rate of ozone production, which when coupled with automobile emissions (and other air pollution sources) increases health risks throughout a metropolitan area. Other studies show that impervious surfaces force stormwater to run off into sewers and forestall the natural cooling effect that occurs as the water evaporates or percolates into the soil. With the causes in mind, the following factors can significantly affect the mitigation of heat islands:

- Lighter-colored building surface materials (especially roofing) and paving materials can reduce heat absorption (fig. 3.33).
- Pervious pavement and exposed ground cover can assist water retention and increase cooling.
- Shading devices (e.g., awnings, canopies, shutters) can help keep surface temperatures cooler by blocking the sun's radiation.
- Trees and ground covers can provide shade and increase evapotranspiration.

These elements may already exist, especially around many older residential and low-rise commercial buildings, or they can be integrated into the proposed rehabilitation and reuse. Aside from the cooling provided by these measures, the retention of water through percolation into the soil allows stormwater to recharge local aquifers, which will reduce costs of stormwater management at local water treatment facilities. These social and economic benefits contribute to the sustainability of the community as a whole.

CHAPTER FOUR

Economic Factors

Throughout the world, policy decisions are based on the economic projections or demonstrated impacts of a market-driven economy. As important as social and environmental considerations may be, the predominant question usually is how well a project pays back in economic terms. Under the current framework that defines success using strictly economic metrics, the philosophy of extraction and depletion and the ongoing demand to produce things quickly and cheaply will prevail. The ideals of social equity and environmental stewardship have held a lesser role in developing new opportunities for growth. In the pervasive economics-based decision system, potential projects must demonstrate an economic return to their investors or a reduced cost to accomplish economic goals. This chapter explores tax credits, grants, and other programs that are available in the United States for preservation and adaptive use projects. The chapter then demonstrates the broader economic implications of success in preserving and reusing buildings using common economic metrics (e.g., property values, job growth and increased tax revenues, increased income, jobs created per $1 million spent, and the cost of each job created). Although many advocates and consumers of cultural heritage do not specifically think in terms of economic benefit, the economic indicators regarding preservation and reuse definitively show significantly better outcomes than other economic incentives and activities.

Economic Incentives

The financing structures for preservation and reuse are multilayered and complex. Markets are difficult to interpret, but increasingly effective incentives for preservation and reuse are being developed. In Europe, the overall financing structure integrated a number of financial instruments and incentive programs into a complicated process that has nonetheless been worth the effort. Learning from European precedents, it is evident that in the United States the collaborative models of professional practice must likewise be extended to include integration of financial institutions and instruments specifically geared toward ensuring stewardship of the built environment through well-tailored funding processes. In the United States, as developers have endeavored to assemble financing from an ever-widening range of sources, conflicting requirements of assorted programs can forestall the initiation or completion of a project. Through trial and error, the network of incentives and financing has been refined, and projects can be structured to mitigate if not eliminate these conflicts. The key is to let the successes (and failures) act as the mechanism to help mature the process and draw new participants into this increasingly sophisticated market. The results of successful preservation and adaptive reuse projects that draw on these resources (e.g., tax incentives, grants) become invaluable when presenting evidence to lenders, policy makers, and property owners.

As mentioned in chapter 1, the decade after the 1976 American Bicentennial saw significant increases in reusing both historic and older buildings. Tax laws became more amenable to retaining buildings by eliminating accelerated depreciation schedules for new buildings and, instead, defining straight-line depreciation schedules (27.5 years for residential and 39 years for commercial buildings). Previously, the accelerated depreciation schedules for new construction were not available for reused buildings, and their removal created more incentives to retain buildings.

The early 1980s saw increases in the syndication of reuse projects to prospective investors. As their popularity grew, the preservation and adaptive use market expanded as skilled craft trades were revitalized, products appropriate to preservation were introduced, and processes to protect historic resources were developed. However, in 1986, the Reagan administration, concerned over passive depreciation losses being used to offset active income of investors, vastly reduced investment opportunities in building projects. Despite the demonstrated multiplier effect that money spent on historic preservation and adaptive use projects had on local economies and quality of life, historic preservation and adaptive use projects were not exempted from this change. Very quickly, financing options declined. Fortunately, the decade also saw the rise of several economic incentives that were untouched by the changes in the tax laws. These include tax credits, grants, and low-interest loans.

Tax Credits

Federal and state governments provide tax credits as a means of encouraging investment growth in specific directions. Tax credits have been made available to promote historic preservation, low-income housing, energy conservation, and numerous other planning goals. Tax credits are introduced to offset the perceived risk associated with an activity and are a significant financial incentive for preserving and reusing buildings. Unlike a tax deduction, a tax credit is a direct one-for-one reduction in the taxes owed to the federal or state government. Each dollar for a tax credit is directly removed from the taxpayer's tax burden (box 4.1).

Tax credits assist the taxpayers' efforts to retain cash or raise equity and assist the taxing authority efforts to promote economic activities. Federal tax credits are uniform nationwide, whereas tax credits in individual states vary in terms of what qualifies and the specific terms of the credit itself. State historic preservation offices (SHPOs) and economic and community development agencies at the state and local government level maintain information clearinghouses that outline which programs are available at the local, state, and federal levels.

Box 4.1

Tax Deduction versus Tax Credit

A tax credit provides greater value to the taxpayer than the same amount designated as a tax deduction. For the calculations, a 28% tax rate is used.

	Tax Deduction	Tax Credit
Gross income	$100,000	$100,000
Deduction	–10,000	N/A
Adjusted gross income	$90,000	$100,000
Tax rate	× 0.28	× 0.28
Tax burden	$25,200	$28,000
Tax credit	N/A	–10,000
Final tax burden	$25,200	$18,000

So as a deduction, the $10,000 yields a tax burden of $25,200, but as a tax credit, it reduces the tax burden to $18,000.

Historic Preservation Tax Credits

The federal Historic Tax Credit (HTC) program (Section 47 of the Internal Revenue Service [IRS] Code) was instituted in 1976 and amended in 1981 and 1986. This program has also been called the Rehabilitation Investment Tax Credit and the Preservation Tax Credit in various publications and documents issued by federal and state agencies. The three agencies responsible for overseeing this program are the SHPO, the National Park Service (NPS), and the IRS.

The historic preservation tax credit is designed to offset some of the reluctance to work with older buildings. Research shows that it typically costs 4 percent less to reuse a building than to build new, with the range in comparative cost running from 12 percent less to 9 percent more than the comparable new construction. In addition, if costs to raze the existing building are included with the construction costs of the new one, then the cost of the rehabilitated building becomes 3 to 16 percent less than the new replacement building (Rypkema 2005: 89). Although continued successes of tax credit projects support these findings, seismic upgrades and substantial changes in use that trigger higher levels of code requirements can increase costs of rehabilitation and preservation. It is therefore critical from a cost perspective to find a new use that is compatible with the original use of the building that may mitigate additional costs that these upgrades and changes would incur.

Because tax credits were originally granted after the project was completed, many potential investors balked at waiting for the full carryforward period to gain the economic benefit of the credits. This gave rise to the syndication of historic preservation tax credits at the start of a project. The syndicator buys tax credits at $0.90–1.00 on the dollar, which provides initial equity toward the financing of the remainder of the project. An overview of the federal HTC system is given in this chapter. For a full description of the requirements, fees, allowances, and specific processes, refer to the SHPO, NPS, and IRS links in appendix B.

The federal HTC system provides two types of tax credit. The first type of HTC (20 percent HTC) allows the taxpayer to reclaim 20 percent of the qualified rehabilitation expenses. This 20 percent HTC is available for certified rehabilitation of a certified historic structure that is depreciable (i.e., used for income generating purposes—office building, apartment building, or other rental property). A certified rehabilitation is one that conforms to the *Standards* (see chapter 2 for a full description). A certified historic structure is a building listed individually in the National Register of Historic Places (NRHP) or a building that contributes to the significance of the historic district in which it is located.

The second type of HTC (10 percent HTC) can be used to reclaim 10 percent of applicable rehabilitation expenses and is used on a nonhistoric depreciable building built before 1936 being rehabilitated for nonresidential purposes. The 10 percent HTC is applied only to buildings that are *not* listed on the NRHP (or any state and local registers). Pre-1936 buildings that are located in a recognized historic district but are designated as "non-contributing" also are eligible. There are additional construction requirements to qualify for this credit as well: Fifty percent of the exterior walls must remain as exterior walls, 75 percent of the existing internal walls must remain in place, and at least 75 percent of the internal structural framework must remain in place (NPS 2009).

Because the goal of the tax credit is to promote financial competitiveness of projects that involve preservation of existing buildings, costs that are directly related to the preservation of the building are considered to be qualified rehabilitation expenditures (QREs). Examples of QREs include the following:

- Rehabilitation costs
- Construction interest and taxes
- Architectural and engineering fees
- Legal and professional fees
- Developers' fees
- General and administrative fees

Costs related to other aspects that do not directly contribute to the preservation of the existing building are not QREs. These include the following:

- Expansion of the building footprint or volume
- Parking and landscaping
- Acquisition costs
- Acquisition interest and taxes
- Realtor's fee
- Sales and marketing costs

This list of inclusions and exclusions requires the project accounting to delineate these costs separately so that only the appropriate qualified costs can be used (Tyler, Ligibel, and Tyler 2009: 252; Department of the Treasury 2002; NPS 2009: 11).

To qualify for the tax credit, the QREs over a 24-month period must exceed the adjusted basis of the building or $5,000, whichever is greater. The adjusted basis is the value that remains after the value of the land, any depreciation, and any capital improvements are taken into account. The adjusted basis is calculated as follows:

Adjusted basis = Initial cost − Land value − Depreciation + Capital improvements.

For example, if the property cost is $200,000, the land value is $120,000, the depreciation taken since the purchase is $12,000, and the capital improvements are $17,000, then the adjusted basis would be $85,000.

Additionally, for a phased project, the 24-month QRE timeframe can be extended to 60 months; however, plans and specifications must be submitted before work begins and must describe all rehabilitation phases.

The SHPO and the NPS are the contact points for marshaling the application through the process. The instructions for the application spell out the various submission requirements that are anticipated. Part 1 ("Evaluation of Significance") includes two major components: a physical description and a statement of why it is significant. In essence, Part 1 is a version of the NRHP nomination process described in chapter 2. If the historic resource is already on the NRHP, reference can be made directly to its original nomination form, and that information is supplemented to include changes that have occurred since that nomination was originally completed. If the resource is not on the NRHP, then the applicant must develop the needed information. The applicant should consult with the SHPO to get a preliminary determination of eligibility for the NRHP. The SHPO will be able to get this under way and send the request to the NPS for the actual determination.

When approval of Part 1 designates the building as a certified historic structure, the building is eligible for the 20 percent HTC and ineligible for the 10 percent HTC. If a building that is not on the NRHP is determined to be eligible for listing, the applicant must submit the final NRHP application within 2 years of completing the project to qualify for the 20 percent HTC.

Part 2 ("Description of Rehabilitation Work") outlines existing conditions and proposed changes. There are three components. The first is a collection of images that show the conditions before the rehabilitation work has started. Next is a detailed list of each proposed change that includes a description of the processes that will be used to achieve them. These descriptions are tied to the last component, which consists of plans, specifications, and manufacturers' product catalog cuts for the project. This is where the applicant must demonstrate that work will be done in accordance with the *Standards*. Part 2 is reviewed by the SHPO. It is good practice to consult with the SHPO as plans and specifications are developed to reveal any potential processes or designs that may cause the application to be rejected. This consultation should also extend to bodies (e.g., the local historic landmarks commission) that have local design review authority. After receiving approvals (typically 30 days for the SHPO and 30 days for the NPS), the project can proceed. Approval of Part 2 constitutes the designation of the proposed work as a certified rehabilitation.

Part 3 ("Request for Certification of Completed Work") outlines the conditions after the project has been completed and consists largely of images and text descriptions that show that the work was done in accordance with the *Standards*. This is submitted to the SHPO, who forwards it to the NPS. Once it is approved, the applicant can file their historic tax credit application with the IRS. Despite the best intentions, occasionally a project will be rejected by the SHPO or the NPS because of something that changed during construction or was misunderstood in Part 2. When this happens, there is an appeals process to determine how the issue can be resolved.

Under the requirements of Internal Revenue Code Section 50(a), there is a tax credit recapture period of 5 years (Internal Revenue Service 2011: 1). After the project has been completed and placed in service, the applicant must retain ownership for 5 years or pay back the credit. The recapture period is prorated such that selling the building in the first year triggers a 100 percent remission of the credit, and this remission is reduced by 20 percent each year until the 5-year window is completed. The NPS has the authority to inspect the property at any time to determine whether any unauthorized renovations have been made. If so, the NPS can revoke the certification and notify the IRS (NPS 2009: 13).

In addition to federal HTCs, state preservation tax credits are also available and vary by state in the percentage of total construction cost and the individual details pertaining to recapture, syndication, and eligibility. These credits have been gaining in popularity at the state level and have been increasingly twinned with federal HTCs when possible. In fiscal year 2009, 37.5 percent of the projects certified by the NPS included the use of state tax credits (NPS 2009: 19).

Despite difficulties with the early versions of Leadership in Energy and Environmental Design (LEED) (as described in chapters 1 and 3), HTCs have been successfully claimed on LEED projects. Among the certified historic buildings that have earned both HTCs and LEED certification (or higher) are the following (Tess 2010; Taylor-Wells 2008: 109–112; NPS 2009: 13; Author's personal notes):

Christman Construction Headquarters, Grand Rapids, Michigan, LEED Triple-Platinum
Gerding Theater (fig. 4.1), Portland, Oregon, LEED Platinum
Nines Hotel, Portland, Oregon, LEED Platinum
Big D Construction Headquarters, Salt Lake City, Utah, LEED Gold
Ecotrust Building, Portland, Oregon, LEED Gold
Balfour-Guthrie, Portland, Oregon, LEED Silver
Scowcroft Building, Ogden, Utah, LEED Silver
A. J. Lindemann & Hoverson Showroom and Warehouse, Chicago, Illinois, LEED Silver

In 2010, other HTC projects seeking LEED certification or higher included the following:

Palomar Hotel, Philadelphia, Pennsylvania
Court Square Center, Memphis, Tennessee
Mercy Corps Headquarters, Portland, Oregon
Deco and Barclay Buildings, Milwaukee, Wisconsin
IBM Building, Chicago, Illinois

As developers look for more cost-effective ways to increase the value of their properties, particularly in economic downturns, the use of HTCs provides a growing opportunity for financing reuse projects.

Although some tax credit programs can be paired ("twinned" or "piggy-backed") with the HTC program, certain provisions, allowances, or require-

Figure 4.1. The Gerding Theater in Portland, Oregon was the first building to attain both LEED Platinum certification and historic preservation tax credits in the United States.

ments may conflict with the *Standards*. Likewise, some tax credit programs such as the Renewable Energy Tax Credit (Section 48 of the Internal Revenue Code) cannot be used with the HTC (Hykan 2009). Federal, state, and local program coordinators administering these programs will be able to indicate at the start of a proposed project where the potential problem areas lie and whether the tax credits can be combined. Two of the more common programs used with the preservation tax credits are the Low-Income Housing Tax Credit (LIHTC) (fig. 4.2) and the New Market Tax Credit (NMTC). Unfortunately, the LIHTC and NMTC cannot be combined, and the LIHTC cannot be used with the 10 percent HTC.

Low-Income Housing Tax Credit

The LIHTC program accounted for nearly 90 percent of the nation's affordable rental housing created in 2006 (Enterprise Community Investment 2006). The program (Section 42 of the Internal Revenue Code) was enacted in 1986 to encourage investment in affordable rental housing. Federal law

Figure 4.2. The Rio Grande Hotel in Salt Lake City, Utah was rehabilitated into a single-room occupancy building using a combination of Historic Tax Credits and Low-Income Housing Tax Credits.

mandates that priority be given to projects serving the lowest-income families and those that will remain affordable for the longest period of time. Federal law also requires that 10 percent of the tax credit allocation be reserved for nonprofit-owned projects.

The IRS annually distributes housing tax credits to state agencies, which award LIHTCs to developers of qualified projects. In 2003, the allocation rate was revised to $1.75 per resident, and a built-in adjustment for annual inflation was added (United States Department of Housing and Urban Development (HUD) 2010a). For 2011, each state's housing tax credit allocation ceiling was $2.15 per resident (Pavao 2011). The allocation pool is created on an annual cycle, but the state has 2 years to dispense each cycle of funding. In this process, however, only the value of the first year of the 10 years of tax credits is used to portion out the allocation pool.

Developers of qualified projects sell the tax credits to investors or syndicators to increase equity and reduce the debt borrowed so that the project can offer lower rents. If the property maintains compliance with program requirements, the investors receive a credit against their federal tax liability every year for 10 years (HUD 2010a). The tax credit can be used to renovate existing or construct new rental buildings. The LIHTC subsidizes either 30 percent or 70 percent of the low-income unit costs in a project. These percentages increase to 39 percent and 91 percent, respectively, in census tracts areas designated by HUD as being in particular need of investment (Rypkema 2002b: 10–11).

The 30 percent subsidy is an automatic 4 percent tax credit that covers the acquisition cost of existing buildings or new construction that uses additional federal subsidies. The 70 percent subsidy is a 9 percent tax credit that supports any new construction built without using funds from other federal subsidies. Eligible rental properties have lower debt service and lower vacancy rates than market-rate rental housing. These properties usually have a quick lease-up and offer strong potential economic returns because of the LIHTC credit. With the help of additional federal, state, and local subsidies, many developers have made these projects financially feasible.

The LIHTC is a complex income tax area, however, and the associated paperwork is extensive. Seeking advice from a tax consultant can ensure a thorough understanding of the process (Affordable Housing Resource Center 2010). According to HUD (2010c), the program requires that a proposed project must

- Be a residential rental property
- Commit to one of two possible low-income occupancy threshold requirements
- Restrict rents, including utility charges, in low-income units
- Operate under the rent and income restrictions for 30 years or longer, pursuant to written agreements with the agency issuing the tax credits

If the developer acquires an existing building, all rehabilitation work must be completed to use it as a residential rental property. Tax credits may be earned on the acquisition of an existing development if the property being acquired has not changed ownership and has been in service during the previous 10 years. Buildings not used in more than 10 years are eligible even if ownership has changed. All projects must meet either of these threshold requirements:

- 20–50 rule: At least 20 percent of the units must be rent restricted and occupied by households with incomes at or below 50 percent of the HUD-determined area median income.

- 40–60 rule: At least 40 percent of the units must be rent restricted and occupied by households with incomes at or below 60 percent of the HUD-determined area median income.

The rent cannot exceed the LIHTC rent limits, which are based on a percentage of area median income; however, the LIHTC program restricts only the rent paid by the tenant and not the total rent of a building. Therefore, rental assistance programs can allow the total rent to be above the LIHTC rent limit while still accommodating a percentage of low-rent units. Additionally, LIHTC housing must have a minimum affordability period of 30 years. This includes a 15-year compliance period and a subsequent 15-year extended use period. The allocating agency monitors compliance during the affordability period and reports the results to the IRS (HUD 2010c).

To determine the tax credit amount, the eligible basis must be calculated. Like HTC projects, LIHTC projects must have a depreciable basis. The eligible costs include construction costs (for the low-income portion only) and other "soft" costs such as architectural and engineering fees, soil tests, and utility connection fees. Nondepreciable costs that are not allowed include the acquisition cost for the land (for new construction projects), permanent financing costs, and initial deposits to reserves.

Next, the applicable fraction is calculated. This fraction is the lower of two percentages: the percentage of qualified low-income units in the project and the percentage of low-income housing square footage in the project. At this point the qualified basis can be determined and adjustments for location (e.g., qualified census tract or difficult development area) are made (HUD 2010a). The developer then uses this to calculate LIHTCs (box 4.2).

New Market Tax Credit

The NMTC program (Section 45D Internal Revenue Code) focuses on creating new business activity in low-income communities. The NMTC is part of the Community Renewal Tax Relief Act of 2000 (NPS 2010a) and is administered by the Department of the Treasury's Community Development Financial Institutions Fund (CDFI Fund). The program is successful in broadening the leverage of foregone tax revenues. The US Treasury reports that every $1 of

Box 4.2

Low-Income Housing Tax Credit Calculation

A developer wants to reuse a former school as an LIHTC project. She proposes to construct thirty-five units, of which 40 percent will be for rent-restricted households. The building is not in a qualified census tract or difficult development area. The project will also be seeking the 20 percent federal Historic Tax Credit (HTC). This application is for the 30 percent subsidy that allows the inclusion of acquisition costs, considers the effect of other federal subsidies, and automatically qualifies for a 4 percent tax credit. The rehabilitation does not expand the building. For simplicity in this example, the eligible LIHTC and HTC soft costs are the same. For a specific project, verify eligibility with the Internal Revenue Service. The tax credit calculations are as follows:

Costs

A. Land acquisition	$500,000
B. Dwelling rehabilitation	2,000,000
C. Site improvements	350,000
D. Architecture and engineering fees	25,000
E. Other eligible soft costs	15,000
F. Total development costs	$2,890,000

Other Federal Subsidies

G. HTC-qualified rehabilitation expenditures (B + D + E)	2,040,000
H. Total 20% HTC (0.20 × G)	408,000

LIHTC Calculation

I. Eligible basis (F − H)	2,482,000
J. Qualified basis (I × 0.40)	992,800
K. Annual credit (0.04 × J)	39,712
L. Total LIHTCs (10 years × K)	397,120
Total of all tax credits	$805,120

The amount of the combined credits may be sold to a syndicator to reduce the overall project cost and in turn lower rental rates.

foregone tax revenues under the NMTC leverages about $12 of private investment in distressed communities on a cost basis (USTREAS 2010b).

For a given project to qualify for funding, the buildings being built or renovated must be in a census tract where the poverty rate is at least 20 percent or where the median family income is 80 percent or less than that of its metropolitan area or state, whichever is less. The NMTC Program has three key objectives:

- To increase the flow of equity capital into entities financing businesses and real estate projects in low-income communities
- To provide capital to low-income community businesses and real estate projects at better rates and terms than would otherwise be available in the marketplace
- To provide jobs, and other goods and services, to residents of low-income communities

The NMTC program encourages investment in low-income communities through equity investments in a designated Community Development Entity (CDE). For federal income tax purposes, a CDE is treated as a domestic corporation or partnership that has a primary mission of serving or providing investment capital for low-income communities (LICs) or low-income people, maintains accountability to LIC residents through representation on any governing board of the entity or any advisory board to the entity, and has been certified as a CDE by the CDFI Fund. The CDE must use all NMTC proceeds for loans and investments in businesses and real estate developments in LICs (USTREAS 2009).

CDEs have used NMTC proceeds to finance a variety of activities in distressed urban and rural communities throughout the United States, including alternative energy companies, charter schools, health care facilities, affordable housing, child care providers, supermarkets, restaurants, museums, hotels, performing arts centers, manufacturers, processors, distributors, business incubators, office buildings, shopping centers, substance abuse treatment facilities, and facilities for the homeless (USTREAS 2010a).

NMTCs are federal income tax credits given for making a qualified equity investment in a designated CDE. The credit equals 39 percent of the investment in a CDE and is claimed over a 7-year period. For the first 3 years, the annual credit is 5 percent of the amount paid for investment. In the final 4 years, the credit is 6 percent annually. Investors may not redeem their investments in the CDE before the 7-year period ends (USTREAS 2010a). For example, a $1 million investment creates a $390,000 NMTC that would be paid out as $50,000 annually for the first 3 years and $60,000 annually for the final 4 years.

The allocations are done annually on competitive basis. The CDFI Fund allocated $3.5 billion in the 2009 application round. This amount was supplemented by $1.5 billion from the American Recovery and Reinvestment Act (USTREAS 2009). Overall, the CDFI Fund is authorized to allocate tax credit authority to support investments, in the aggregate, of $26 billion (USTREAS 2010a). Additionally, NMTCs can be combined with HTCs that are not used for residential purposes (fig. 4.3), with the exception of hotels, which are considered a commercial activity.

Figure 4.3. The financing for the reuse of the former First Security Bank building in Salt Lake City, Utah combined New Market Tax Credits and Historic Tax Credits.

The National Trust Community Investment Corporation (NTCIC), a certified development enterprise, described the projects listed in table 4.1 in its portfolio (NTCIC 2005), for which it has developed tax credit financing. These projects used NMTCs and HTCs together to raise equity for the financing of the project. NTCIC also reported on the number of new construction and permanent jobs created and the new state and local taxes generated.

From this discussion you can see that tax credits can be used to foster the goals of stewardship of the built environment by reducing the risks associated with preserving and adaptively using existing buildings. The expected tax credits can be syndicated to develop much-needed upfront equity or to pass along cost savings accrued to the occupant and community in the form of lower rent or better amenities that enhance the community.

Grants

There are a variety of grant programs that provide cash to assist in reusing an existing building. Like tax credits, they are designed to promote specific economic activities that either directly or indirectly promote stewardship of the built environment. Although fewer grants are actually geared toward construction (often called bricks-and-mortar grants), a number of grants can be used in the planning and design stages and for retrofitting existing buildings. These grants may be a full cash award or may require matching funding (e.g., $1 from the applicant for each $1 awarded from the granting organization) or donation of in-kind services. In particular, the Community Development Block Grant (CDBG), the Energy Efficiency and Conservation Block Grant, the Certified Local Government Grant, and the Save America's Treasures grant programs are relevant to projects involving the reuse and preservation of buildings.

The Housing and Community Development Act of 1974 enabled HUD to start the CDBG program to provide communities with resources to address their unique community development needs; to ensure decent, affordable housing and neighborhood revitalization; to provide services in communities; and to create jobs.

HUD awards CDBG grants directly to state and local governments, which then define how they distribute those funds in accordance with HUD requirements. The program provides grants to 1,180 units of local government and

Table 4.1

National Trust Community Investment Corporation Projects That Have Combined Historic Tax Credits and New Market Tax Credits

Project Name and Location	Cost ($M)	Area (ksf)	Tax Credits ($M)	New Jobs	New Taxes ($M)
Arthur C. Flemming Building, Washington, DC	3.1	7.2	0.6	209	0.6
Triangle Biology Center, Durham, North Carolina	3.8	18.4	0.8	373	0.7
Professional Building, Suffolk, Virginia	5.3	35.6	1.3	585	0.9
Heimann Building, San Antonio, Texas	5.9	20.1	0.8	740	1.2
Dalton Building and Annex, Baltimore, Maryland	6.8	35.0	1.0	421	1.4
Arbaugh Building, Lansing, Michigan	8.2	58.2	1.7	989	1.8
80 Fourth Avenue, New York, New York	8.6	26.7	1.1	424	1.7
Wheeling Stamping Building, Wheeling, West Virginia	9.9	94.0	1.1	1,491	2.0
Telegram Building, Portland, Oregon	11.5	31.4	2.1	726	2.2
First Security Bank, Salt Lake City, Utah	20.8	158.5	2.8	2,842	4.3
Masonic Temple, Baltimore, Maryland	21.4	90.0	6.3	2,748	4.5
Tennessee Theater, Knoxville, Tennessee	29.4	60.0	6.1	1,640	6.1
Dia:Beacon, Beacon, New York	31.4	292.0	6.0	3,727	6.0
Peerless Building, Providence, Rhode Island	33.5	209.0	7.2	3,120	6.8
Old Post Office, St. Louis, Missouri	51.2	242	22.9	4,362	8.0
American Tobacco Factory, Durham, North Carolina	63.7	900.0	19.4	9,268	12.7
The Hippodrome, Baltimore, Maryland	71.0	170.0	10.3	4,157	14.3
Coltsville, Hartford, Connecticut	105.6	683.4	19.4	10,057	17.4

These projects are listed from lowest cost to highest cost and together represent a cross-section of sizes and locations nationwide. Overall, the New Market Tax Credit program has provided significant opportunities for business development in economically distressed communities.

states, respectively called entitlement and non-entitlement communities. Entitlement communities are central cities of metropolitan statistical areas with populations of at least 50,000 and qualified urban counties with a population of 200,000 or more. States provide CDBG funds only to non-entitlement communities that have smaller populations than entitlement communities.

HUD calculates each grant amount based on the population, extent of poverty, overcrowding, housing age, and population growth relationship to other metropolitan statistical areas. The allocation nationwide is 70 percent to entitlement communities and 30 percent to non-entitlement communities. In fiscal year 2011, the CDBG allocation was $3.99 billion (United States Office of Management and Budget 2011: 86). At least 70 percent of CDBG funds must benefit low- and moderate-income people and must act toward eliminating blight or addressing community needs to reduce immediate and serious threats to the community where other funding is unavailable. Because reuse projects often achieve these goals, they are a natural fit for the program requirements.

Some state and local governments accept applications on a continuing basis, and others impose specific deadlines. In either event, they must develop an overall plan that defines the eligible activities and projects. The plan must allow and encourage citizen involvement, which is an integral component intended to encourage participation by people of low or moderate income in particular. As described by HUD, the plan must include

> reasonable and timely access to local meetings; an opportunity to review proposed activities and program performance; provide for timely written answers to written complaints and grievances; and identify how the needs of non–English speaking residents will be met in the case of public hearings where a significant number of non–English speaking residents can be reasonably expected to participate. (NPS 2011c)

Selection criteria are established in each state or local government's implementation plan. CDBG funds may be used for acquiring real property, rehabilitating buildings, completing planning activities, improving public facilities, assisting profit-motivated businesses in their economic development and job creation or retention efforts, retrofitting buildings to conserve energy, and relocating or demolishing buildings (NPS 2011c; Salt Lake City 2009; HUD 2009).

The Energy Efficiency and Conservation Block Grant (EECBG) program, funded by the American Recovery and Reinvestment Act of 2009 (Recovery Act), emphasizes the federal priority to use the cheapest, cleanest, and most reliable energy technologies available (e.g., energy efficiency and conservation) nationwide. The program (Title V, Subtitle E of the Energy Independence and

Security Act) was signed into law in 2007 and was modeled after the CDBG program administered by HUD. The EECBG program seeks to help US cities, counties, states, territories, and Indian tribes to develop, promote, implement, and manage energy efficiency and conservation projects and programs that reduce fossil fuel emissions; reduce the total energy use of the eligible entities; improve energy efficiency in the transportation, building, and other appropriate sectors; and create and retain jobs. The program uses formulas and competitive grants to empower applicants to make strategic investments designed to achieve the national long-term goals for energy independence and climate change leadership.

The Recovery Act funding for the EECBG Program provides $3.2 billion. About $2.7 billion of these funds will be awarded through formula grants. Another $454 million will be released as competitive grants. The remainder will go to developing technical assistance tools for grantees. Grants are to be used for energy efficiency and conservation programs and projects and for renewable energy installations on government buildings. Eligible activities include the following:

- Developing energy efficiency and conservation strategies
- Completing building energy audits and retrofits, including weatherization
- Developing financial incentive programs for energy efficiency such as energy savings performance contracting, on-bill financing, and revolving loan funds
- Defining transportation programs to conserve energy
- Creating building code, implementation, and inspection processes
- Installing distributed energy technologies such as combined heat and power and district heating and cooling systems
- Creating material conservation programs such as source reduction, recycling, and recycled content procurement programs
- Reducing and capturing greenhouse gas emissions generated by landfills or similar waste-related sources
- Installing energy-efficient traffic signals and street lighting
- Installing renewable energy technologies on government buildings
- Completing other appropriate activities that meet the intent of the program and are approved by the US Department of Energy (USDOE 2009)

The EECBG program is part of a group of programs that also includes the Weatherization Assistance Program and the State Energy Program, which is monitored by the Office of Energy Efficiency and Renewable Energy Weatherization and Intergovernmental Program. Approximately 2,300 cities, counties, and Native American tribes were designated to receive an EECBG to develop and implement projects to improve energy efficiency and reduce energy use and fossil fuel emissions in their communities (USDOE 2010a). More up-to-date information should be available from respective State Energy Offices.

A Certified Local Government (CLG) is a partnership between local, state, and national governments that focuses on promoting historic preservation at the grassroots level. First, the local community government must complete a certification process to become a CLG. CLGs are funded by the Historic Preservation Fund (HPF), a federal grant program appropriated by Congress and administered by the NPS to provide financial support to the SHPOs. Under the provisions of the NHPA, SHPOs are then required to award at least 10 percent of their annual HPF funding in the form of CLG grants. The HPF grants to CLGs fund a range of local historic preservation projects. Each year, the SHPO defines the criteria used to select projects for funding. CLG projects have typically included the following:

- Completing architectural, historical, and archeological surveys and oral histories
- Preparing nominations to the National Register of Historic Places
- Researching and developing historic context information
- Working for historic preservation commissions
- Writing or amending preservation ordinances
- Preparing preservation plans
- Publishing information and education activities
- Publishing historic site inventories
- Developing publication of walking and driving tours
- Developing slide or tape shows, videotapes
- Training commission members and staff
- Developing architectural drawings and specifications
- Preparing façade studies or condition assessments
- Rehabilitating or restoring properties listed in the NRHP

All CLG grants produce a completed, tangible product or measurable result, and all must be carried out in accordance with the applicable *Standards*. The funding for a CLG grant must be sufficient to have tangible results, but aside from that, there are no specific requirements regarding the amount of grant money SHPOs make available to CLGs. The monetary value tends to be small, especially when there are many CLGs statewide, except in states where the SHPOs award fewer but larger grants. The NPS reported in 2001 that CLG grants were as low as $500 and as high as $60,000 (NPS 2010b), but in recent years these levels have dropped. For example, in New York, in 2010, CLG grants were reported as mostly in the $5,000–15,000 range (New York State Office of Parks, Recreation & Historic Preservation 2011). In California, the range for CLG grant funding for 2011–2012 is $5,000–22,500 (Office of Historic Preservation 2011). In most states, CLG grants are matching grants for which recipients provide a certain amount of cash or in-kind services to complement the amount of grant money. Although each SHPO decides what match amount is required, it is often a dollar-for-dollar requirement; that is, for every dollar awarded, the applicant must provide a matching dollar in services, cash, or volunteer hours (NPS 2010b). Specific details of the CLG grant program in each state or community are available from the SHPO or local planning department.

The Save America's Treasures (SAT) federal grant program was established by executive order in 1998 and was closed due to funding cuts in 2011. However, had the program continued and even expanded, the potential economic impacts were of such a compelling nature that they are reported here for comparison to other economic development tools. Although no new project applications are being accepted, projects already funded will continue to their expected completion. The program's goals were to foster pride in American heritage (fig. 4.4), educate Americans about preservation problems, raise concern for preservation needs, and stimulate public involvement. The NPS administered the program in collaboration with the President's Committee on the Arts and the Humanities, the Institute of Museum and Library Services, the National Endowment for the Arts, and the National Endowment for the Humanities (NTHP 2010c).

These annual grants were offered for preservation or conservation work on historic collections and properties. Collections include documents, archives, sculptures, and works of art. Properties include historic districts, sites,

Figure 4.4. The Save America's Treasures program awarded a $250,000 grant to help restore and convert the 1806 Prudhomme-Rouquier House in Natchitoches, Louisiana to a meeting and conference center (Dono 2010).

buildings, structures, and objects. Grants were awarded through a competitive process and required a dollar-for-dollar match. The minimum grant request for collection projects was $25,000 federal share; the minimum grant request for historic property projects was $125,000 federal share. The maximum grant request for all projects was $700,000 federal share. In 2008, the average federal grant award to historic properties was $279,000 (NPS 2011c). The program was open to a broad spectrum of applicants, including the following:

- Federal agencies funded by the Department of the Interior and Related Agencies Appropriations Act
- Federal agencies collaborating with a nonprofit partner to preserve the historic properties owned by the federal agency, which submit applications through the nonprofit partner
- Nonprofit, tax-exempt 501(c) US organizations
- Units of state or local government
- Federally recognized Indian tribes
- Historic properties associated with active religious organizations

Acceptable projects were focused on preservation or conservation work on nationally significant historic structures and sites. Historic structures and sites include historic districts, sites, buildings, structures, and objects. The selection criteria for applications dictated that the historic property must have been both nationally significant and either threatened or endangered. The proposed project must have substantially mitigated the threat, must have had a clear public benefit, and must have been able to be completed within the scope, schedule, and budget described in the application. The application itself needed to include a description of the process planned for obtaining the requisite nonfederal match (NPS 2011c). Some successful projects included work on the Acoma Pueblo, Lincoln Cottage, and Frank Lloyd Wright's studio, Taliesin (NTHP 2010c). Types of projects that did not qualify for funding include the following (NPS 2010c):

- Acquisition of historic sites, buildings, structures, or objects
- Survey or inventory of historic properties or cataloging of collections
- Long-term maintenance or curatorial work beyond the grant period
- Interpretive or training programs
- Reconstruction of historic properties
- Moving historic properties or work on historic properties that have been moved
- Construction of new buildings
- Historic structure reports and condition assessments, unless they are one component of a larger project to perform work recommended by these studies
- Cash reserves, endowments, or revolving funds. Funds must be expended within the grant period, which is generally 2 to 3 years
- Costs of fundraising campaigns
- Costs of work performed before announcement of award
- For federal agency grantees, federal salaries, agency overhead, or administrative costs

This program complemented the other grant programs described earlier. NTHP president Richard Moe once described this program as "the country's most significant preservation effort in over 50 years" (NTHP 2010c). SAT encouraged the rehabilitation of historically significant buildings. Since

1998, SAT has been credited with creating approximately seventy-two new jobs per $1 million spent, which compared quite favorably with more conventional economic activities and was especially favorable when compared with the American Recovery and Reinvestment Act of 2009, commonly called the "Stimulus Package," which created only four new jobs per $1 million spent. By 2009, the SAT program had allocated approximately $220 million dollars for the restoration of nearly 900 historic structures. The SAT program funding had generated more than $330 million in funds from other sources and created 16,012 jobs. The cost per job created was $13,780 (Rypkema 2010). Whether the funding cuts were made because of its small profile at the national level or a lack of understanding as to the program's potentially broader impact, the loss of the SAT program is representative of the lack of awareness of what preservation and reuse can do for economic development.

Closer attention to the finer points of each program is beyond the scope of this book. However, one must pay careful attention to which programs complement or conflict with one another when seeking funding assistance. As with the tax credits, the best approach is to work collaboratively with the people directly in charge of the processes and communicate effectively between the various agencies.

Economic Planning and Development Tools

In addition to tax credits and grants, a number of other strategies and incentives are available. Many of these are tools available to local and state governments. Most common are the Redevelopment Authority and the Office of Economic and Community Development programs, which vary by state and local government. As can be seen from the discussion on grants, a great variety of funding is available from the federal government via these programs.

Of particular relevance are the planning tools available to promote reinvestment in buildings and communities. These include incentives such as tax increment financing (TIF), tax abatements, and transfer of development rights.

TIF is a process in which the community designates certain districts as a redevelopment area. In implementing the TIF process, the community defines the property tax level baseline for the predevelopment conditions and then commits to construct infrastructure improvements, which then attract redevelopment (both new construction and rehabilitation). The increased taxes generated above the baseline are recouped by transferring those specific tax revenues to fund infrastructure improvements. Similarly, some communities have tax abatement programs that will reduce the tax burden or eliminate the property taxes altogether to entice redevelopment activities.

The third tool, transfer of development rights, provides a means to reduce development pressures on older and historic properties (as well as open lands) by allowing a property owner to sell or transfer the development rights to another property owner or property where higher density or a taller building with a greater floor area ratio (FAR) is desired. This usually occurs in cities trying to protect historic buildings located in places where the smaller scale of an older building, when compared with those around it, makes it attractive to developers to raze the buildings and build anew.

Economic Indicators

To establish a baseline for measuring the success of redevelopment efforts, the commonly used parameters are property values, job growth and tax revenues, and revitalized communities. From a stewardship perspective, success is achieved in creating a holistic sense of community, but economic impacts are more easily measured and therefore frequently used to describe success (or failure) in comparable terms.

Property Values

Property rights are a concern for many property owners. Therefore, one constant anxiety that arises when the talk of creating historic districts begins is the perception that the additional regulations that accompany local designation and oversight will somehow impede the appreciation of property values. This myth abounds nationwide. The truth is that a multitude of studies on the economic impact of historic district designations show that at the very least, the designated districts appreciate similarly to properties in adjoining undesignated neighborhoods. More often, however, properties in the designated district appreciate much faster than similar properties in adjoining undesignated neighborhoods.

The misperception arises when property owners fail to understand that there is a market for buildings (fig. 4.5) that are recognized for their historic qualities; exist in an interesting and architecturally diverse neighborhood; have good proximity to local businesses, cultural events, and institutions; can promote opportunities for less dependence on the automobile through shorter commuting distances, public transit, or walkable distances to local businesses; and have a sense of community.

These are the features that many historic districts may already have before designation or continue to develop afterward. The incentives described throughout this book also play an important role in fostering these qualities. The primary incentives for property owners to increase their holdings in historic districts are the tax credits and grants that can accrue to the owner in his or her efforts to improve the property. Although it may not seem that way, the design review authority granted to the local landmarks commission is intended to spur on higher-quality rehabilitation work. The design standards in both the *Standards* and the local district guidelines are in place to ensure that the improvements do not adversely affect the very characteristics that define the neighborhood in the first place. In many cases, reviews look at demolition, materials, and changes in massing, height, or form to ensure that the rehabilitation work is compatible with the existing buildings around it. Restrictions of this kind rarely inhibit economic development.

Job Growth and Tax Revenues

In the early twenty-first century, two parameters have become the central indicators of the economic success of a program: the job growth spurred by the program and the tax revenues gained. The *Federal Tax Incentives for Rehabilitating Historic Buildings: Statistical Report and Analysis for Fiscal Year 2009* states that from 1977 to 2009, HTC programs have created a nominal (not adjusted for inflation) $55.5 billion in historic preservation activity (NPS 2010a: 2). The *Second Annual Report of the Economic Impact of the Federal Historic Tax Credit* further reveals that in fiscal year 2010 dollars (adjusted for inflation) for the period 1978–2010, the preservation tax credit program has generated $90.4 billion in rehabilitation activity at a cost of $17.5 billion in tax credits (a leverage of more than 5:1) and has created 2,020,800 jobs (which translates to a cost of $8,660 per job) that in turn generated an additional $210.2 billion in

Figure 4.5. The Allegheny West Historic District is in Pittsburgh, Pennsylvania. The buildings date from the nineteenth century, and there are numerous locally owned businesses (e.g., shops, services, restaurants). The district is immediately adjacent to several cultural, sports, and recreational venues located in the Pittsburgh central business district.

output, $76.3 billion in income, $103.8 billion in gross domestic product, and $30.5 billion in tax revenues (Listokin and Lahr 2011: 3–11). As noted earlier, the Recovery Act created only four jobs per million dollars spent, a cost of $250,000 per job created (Rypkema 2010). Each job created was the equivalent of a full-time job for 1 year in which salaries are competitive within the local market for that particular type of job. Overall these figures reflect how expensive it is to create a job using the various strategies being described. Thus, $13,780/job and $8,660/job, respectively, for the Save America's Treasures program and the Historic Tax Credit program are vastly less than the $250,000/job that the stimulus program cost. When coupled with the multiplier effect created as the salaries are spent locally, these new jobs significantly increase the social and economic vitality of the community where the jobs are located. These data reveal that job creation through preservation-oriented programs is cost effective when compared with more highly publicized economic development programs.

The National Conference of State Historic Preservation Officers (NCSHPO 2010) reports that the restoration and rehabilitation of buildings and revitalization of communities are a multi-billion-dollar industry. This industry provides jobs for the entire spectrum of participants involved in the planning, design, construction, operation, and asset management of buildings. As the number of neighborhoods being revitalized grows and the number of new tax-paying residents increases, more retail establishments and tradespeople are needed to sustain them. According to the Advisory Council on Historic Preservation,

> One million dollars spent on rehabilitation, compared to the same amount spent on new construction yields between 5 and 9 more local construction jobs, creates 4.7 more new jobs elsewhere in the community and provides $107,000 more in community income. It also generates $34,000 more in retail sales.

In *The Economics of Historic Preservation: A Community Leader's Guide*, Donovan Rypkema takes this metric one step further by comparing the job creation potential of historic preservation against the primary job sources for a selection of states from across the country (Rypkema 2005: 11). He notes that at the state level, $1 million spent on building rehabilitation created

- 5 more jobs than $1 million for manufacturing electronic equipment in California
- 12 more jobs than $1 million for manufacturing cars in Michigan
- 29 more jobs than pumping $1 million worth of oil in Oklahoma
- 22 more jobs than $1 million for cutting timber in Oregon
- 12 more jobs than $1 million for processing steel in Pennsylvania
- 8 more jobs than $1 million for manufacturing textiles in South Carolina
- 17 more jobs than $1 million for agriculture in South Dakota
- 20 more jobs than $1 million for mining coal in West Virginia

Thus, it can be said that historic preservation is a significant generator of jobs even when compared with the industry for which a state is a recognized leader. Rypkema has also stated that because preservation and rehabilitation are more labor intensive, the jobs can be retained in perpetuity if communities rehabilitate 2–3 percent of their building stock annually (Mize 2009).

Because historic rehabilitation relies more on labor but uses fewer materials than new construction, it contains the multiplier effect generated when money that makes up the wage earners' pay cycles through the community as the wage earner buys goods and services in the community. The local merchants and service providers in turn pay their employees, who perpetuate the cycle. For example, the National Main Street Center (NMSC 2010b) reports that each dollar spent operating a local Main Street program generated $40.35 in return to the community. Although the job creation results themselves are impressive, this multiplier effect is surprising to many and demonstrates the extent of the recirculation of money that can occur.

When money stays within the local economy, the community becomes more economically sustainable. Recognition of this has prompted the emerging trend of buying local. A number of studies show that buying from an independent locally owned business rather than a nationally owned business results in a greater benefit to the economic base of the community (Sustainable Communities 2010).

Almost a decade ago, Elizabeth A. Lyon, the Georgia state historic preservation officer, described the essential qualities of a successful community as follows:

> Successful communities . . . convey a sense of pride and a vision of what they can be. They value quality development based on appreciation for the natural and historic resources that give them distinctiveness. They maintain active economic development programs. Strong traditional institutions and active quality-of-life lobbies are present. They are willing to seek help from the outside, but look to hometown heroes and realize they must help themselves. (Lyon 1993)

This description is still accurate. In the intervening years, many communities have successfully transformed themselves to meet this description, through support from the NMSC Main Street program. Although not every community revitalization effort falls under the auspices of this program, the statistical data associated with it provide valuable insight into the potential benefits that can be attained through its approach to revitalization. In appraising the impact of the Main Street program, Donovan Rypkema (2008) stated,

In the last 25 years, some 1,700 communities in all 50 states have had Main
Street programs. . . . [T]he total amount of public and private reinvestment in
those Main Street communities has been $23 billion. There have been over
67,000 net new businesses created, generating nearly 310,000 net new jobs.
There have been 107,000 building renovations. Every dollar invested in a local
Main Street program leveraged nearly $27 of other investment. The average
cost per job generated—$2,500—is less than a *tenth* of what many state eco-
nomic development programs brag about.

This is strong evidence of the success of a stewardship of the built environment approach overall, but success in the social context of creating new
businesses and jobs is a compelling and yet often overlooked aspect of preservation. Rypkema (2008) concludes that this program is "the most cost-effective
U.S. program for economic development—not just for historic preservation or
downtown revitalization, but the most cost-effective economic development
program *of any kind.*"

In addition to fostering a vibrant economy using local dollars, historically
significant areas can also attract visitors interested in cultural heritage tourism,
a recent trend spurred by increased interest in seeking out places that rein-
force pride in national heritage or introduce diverse local and regional cultures,
traditions, and perspectives. The Heritage Tourism Program of the NTHP
reports that benefits of cultural heritage tourism have a tremendous economic
impact on local economies, including economic benefits such as new businesses, jobs, and higher property values. It improves the quality of life and
promotes community pride.

An area that attracts cultural heritage tourism creates new opportunities for
visitors to understand an unfamiliar place, people, or time. With these visitors
come new opportunities for preservation as well-interpreted sites teach visitors
their importance and, by extension, the importance of preserving other such
sites elsewhere. Perhaps the biggest benefit of cultural heritage tourism is that
opportunities increase for economic diversity, ways to prosper economically
while holding on to the characteristics that make communities special (Cultur-
alheritagetourism.org 2011). The impact of these activities on local economies
is substantial.

In the first large-scale estimate of the size and scope of cultural tourism in
Indiana, the Ball State Center for Business and Economic Research stated in

their report *Cultural Tourism in Indiana: The Impact and Clustering of the Arts and Creative Activities in this Recession* that in 2008 these activities accounted for more than $6.17 billion in economic activity that directly employed more than 53,924 workers. The report further states that these activities generated more than $2.1 billion in value-added production and paid $53.3 million in business-related taxes. In economic terms, these activities also generate indirect and induced increases as money circulates through the local economy. Taking this into account, the impact expands to $11.26 billion in economic activity, 99,935 workers, $4.67 billion in value-added production, and $276.4 million in business-related taxes. The multipliers for these categories—dollar return per dollar invested—were 1.8, 1.9, 2.2, and 5.2, respectively, and imply the relative reach of the activity in the overall economy. In analyzing the data, the authors also noted that the economic activity between 2006 and 2008 increased despite the effects of the recession (Center for Business and Economic Research 2009: 6).

Cultural heritage tourism destinations also include National Heritage Areas (NHAs), as designated by the NPS. These destinations provide a broader cultural range of heritage-oriented activities such as living history farms, museums, festivals, and cultural events. The NPS reports that NHA designation has tangible and intangible benefits. Heritage conservation efforts are grounded in residents' interest and involvement in retaining and interpreting the landscape for future generations and in a community's pride in its history and traditions. The designation fosters a collaborative approach to conservation that does not remove traditional local use and control over the landscape. Designation also comes with limited financial and technical assistance from the NPS. There are currently 49 NHAs across the country (NPS 2011a).

On a national basis, the Association of National Heritage Areas (2006) reported that the network of twenty-seven NHAs generated $8.5 billion in direct and indirect sales, which created an estimated 152,324 jobs and paid $3.2 billion in wages and salaries. By their estimate, the total direct and indirect value added to the community in the form of personal income to workers, profits and rents to businesses, and indirect business taxes paid reached $5 billion.

Beyond generating new jobs and businesses and increasing property values, heritage tourism builds community pride, which in turn improves the quality of life. The main benefits of heritage tourism are stronger local economies and preservation of a community's unique character (NCSHPO 2010). In 2009, domestic and international travelers spent $704 billion in direct travel spending the United States. This generated more than 7.4 million jobs directly, $186 billion in payroll income, and $111 billion in tax revenues for federal, state, and local governments (United States Travel Association 2010). The United States Travel Association has compiled the following comparison of travel characteristics of heritage tourists to other tourists (Texas Historical Commission 2007: 7). In comparison to other tourists, cultural heritage tourists

- Shop more (44 percent versus 33 percent)
- Stay longer (4.7 nights versus 3.4 nights)
- Stay in commercial accommodations more than with family or friends (62 percent versus 56 percent)
- Spend more per trip ($623 versus $457, excluding the cost of transportation)
- Spend more per day ($103.50 versus $81.20)

These figures provide compelling evidence that promoting heritage tourism can be a significant strategy to build up the economic base of a community. All in all, historic preservation fueled by such support as the HTC program, the various grants programs, the Main Street program, and investments supporting cultural heritage tourism is a powerful development tool that can elevate the economic sustainability of a community, town, city, region, or state.

CHAPTER FIVE

Putting It All Together

Revitalization as a first step toward greater sustainability does not occur overnight. The urban renewal projects of the 1960s and 1970s that failed to produce what they were intended to do are prime evidence of that. As Roberta Brandes Gratz notes in *The Battle for Gotham: New York in the Shadow of Robert Moses and Jane Jacobs*, most planners and government officials "don't give credence to the gradual block-by-block and business-by-business improvements that mark organic incrementalism" (Gratz 2010: 203). This lack of credence affects the entire industry spectrum of financing, designing, constructing, owning, and operating buildings. The outcome and implications of incremental growth are often undetected as they occur but are clearly evident when viewed over the long term. In this fashion, many preservation and reuse projects often start on a small, local scale and build outward to surrounding buildings, neighborhoods, and business districts.

The examples of and strategies for stewardship of the built environment cited thus far have demonstrated that the successful preservation and reuse of buildings presents an opportunity to redefine social, environmental, and economic perceptions. Despite being a small segment of the construction industry today, preservation and reuse projects have continued to increase in popularity over the past few years, partially because of

- Emerging social awareness of the lifestyle benefits of living and working in neighborhoods and business districts that create a sense of vitality and a connection to place
- Growing recognition that existing buildings may include energy-efficient features and that tearing down and replacing existing buildings is not sustainable
- Growing recognition that preservation and reuse can provide effective economic stimulation at the community, state, and regional scales

This chapter presents three iconic examples of how preservation and reuse come together to improve the social, environmental, and economic aspects of sustainability. The first, Fort Douglas in Salt Lake City, Utah, illustrates the social opportunity for creating an enhanced sense of place from a collection of underused buildings. This could readily mirror the opportunities for locales that have underused manufacturing facilities available in a contiguous setting. The second, the Christman Building in Lansing, Michigan, the first existing building to earn LEED Triple Platinum accreditation, demonstrates how amenable existing buildings can be to environmental quality and sustainability. Lastly, the Old Post Office in St. Louis demonstrates how a collaborative effort created an economic engine that has spurred on significant rehabilitation in the adjoining blocks. The chapter concludes with a summation of the lessons learned and an outline for the future directions and imperatives that will accelerate the adoption of stewardship of the built environment as a sustainability strategy.

Creating Community: Fort Douglas, Salt Lake City, Utah

In the late twentieth century and even more so in the twenty-first century, many domestic industries were downsized because of offshore competition and weakened economic conditions. This left numerous vacant manufacturing buildings, and by extension the residential and commercial districts supporting them, vulnerable to accelerated decline. This decline has created a dilemma for community leaders as they strive to facilitate the continued sustainability and economic stability of their communities. Several successful large-scale examples provide guidance for possible courses of action. Somewhat surprisingly, these examples are the successful preservation and reuse of decommissioned military bases. Before the war on terrorism, one recurring activity that had a tremendous potential negative impact on local communities was the consolidation of military operations. This consolidation caused the closure and downsizing of numerous bases and military facilities and provided a multitude of simultaneous adaptive reuse opportunities for many older and historic buildings within a singular location. The Base Realignment and Closure Commission transferred decommissioned military facilities to the public sector for reuse. Three notable examples are the Presidio in San Francisco,

California, which has become a major incubator for small business and non-profit institutions; Fort Ord near Monterey, California, which has been converted into the Monterey Peninsula College; and Fort Stephen A. Douglas in Salt Lake City, Utah, which has become a critical component of the educational mission of the University of Utah. All three projects underwent significant planning periods to enable potential users to fully comprehend the demands that such a conversion requires, and their success over the past decade illustrates the longer-term impacts of the conversions. The following case study (Young 2004a: 205–209) focuses on the efforts at the University of Utah to create a "Living and Learning Community" at Fort Stephen A. Douglas.

Once potentially considered part of a primary route for a section of interstate highway, Fort Stephen A. Douglas now has a renewed life. The fort is on the east bench in the foothills immediately adjacent to the University of Utah in Salt Lake City and is a showplace for how to preserve and reuse an assemblage of vacant or underused buildings.

Originally established in 1862, the fort continued to grow throughout the nineteenth century and reached its zenith during World War II. The postwar period saw a long, slow decline, and eventually the fort shrank to a reserve center headquarters. The historic core of the fort was designated as a National Historic Landmark in 1970, by which time the US Army had ceded most of its original 10,525 acres to the University of Utah for academic, administrative, and residential facilities or transferred it to the National Guard, Veterans Administration, and the National Forest Service. The university used the opportunity as host of the 2002 Olympic Athletes' Village to resolve a shortfall in its student residential accommodations and broaden the use of the fort as a "Living and Learning Community" where residential, teaching, and research activities could bring renewed life to the fort (fig. 5.1).

The University of Utah has reused the existing residential and administrative buildings of the fort for student housing, small classroom spaces, and research centers. The project encompasses forty buildings on approximately 63 acres. Although early work included converting several small housing units on "Officer's Circle" into housing for students in a scholarship program, the university had a larger goal to use the entire fort as a residential and scholastic environment that would facilitate better integration of students' social and academic activities. The University of Utah used the opportunity of the 2002 Winter Olympics to improve its dormitory housing while meeting the

Figure 5.1. Fort Douglas, site of the 2002 Olympic Athletes' Village, in Salt Lake City, Utah, serves as home to the University of Utah's "Living and Learning Community."

need for accommodations for 2,500 athletes. The university removed nonhistoric buildings and used vacant space to construct dormitories and a hotel that provides housing for guests of the University of Utah, conference rooms, and meeting spaces.

As a National Historic Landmark, Fort Douglas is protected by the strictest preservation regulations. This factor led the university to undertake a planning study to ensure that infill buildings would not adversely affect the composition and form of the fort and its environment. Overall, and in the larger context, this planning process was conducted as part of developing and refining a long-range development plan for the entire university. To accomplish this, the university convened a steering committee comprised of various interested parties from the local community, including representatives from the university, the army, local citizens, and other state agencies (e.g., the state historic preservation office, the governor's office). A planning consultant was hired and spent 2 years convening numerous meetings to coordinate the needs of the university with the demands of the Salt Lake Olympic Committee and the requirements of the *Secretary of the Interior's Standards* as overseen by the Utah state historic preservation officer. Anne Racer, director of facilities planning, characterized the philosophy of collaborative participation as unique and further stated, "We approached the project with the idea that people who are actively involved in developing a plan are more likely to accept it, adopt it, and use it" (Racer 2002: 2). The process included the following phases:

1. Programming and need assessment: The planning consultant interviewed and coordinated the information flow between all concerned parties, made preliminary visual studies to educate these parties on the potential impacts of their needs, and identified housing and operational support requirements.

2. Identification and physical exploration of existing facilities: A local architectural firm investigated the physical condition of the buildings, identified the historic aspects of the buildings to establish a baseline for the historic rehabilitation work, prepared a cost estimate for the rehabilitation of each building and any infrastructure modification and extension costs, and prepared an overall cost estimate.

3. Schematic design development: The project team identified significant buildings and spaces where infill buildings could be built, developed several schematic designs using a material palette based on existing building, and coordinated resource allocations to develop a overall budget.

4. Schematic design review and modification: The interested parties reviewed the alternatives and selected a final design based on modifications to get the project within the $120 million budgetary constraints of the state legislature.

5. Construction document development: The team then developed the project plans into construction documents.

6. Bid submission and contractor selections: The team sent the project out to bids and selected the contractors.

7. Construction: The construction period took approximately 2 years.

8. Occupation: The Salt Lake Olympic Committee required that the buildings be commissioned and in operation for at least 12 months before the 2002 Games so that operational problems could be detected and remedied. As part of a commissioning process, this phase enabled plant operations to engage in the use and maintenance of the buildings before the Olympics.

As a result, the project was recognized in 1999 as an Official Save America's Treasures Project, and it has continued to receive honors and awards. In 2001 it received an Honor Award from the Society for College and University Planning and the American Institute of Architects and culminated with a Preservation Award in October 2001 from the National Trust for Historic Preservation (NTHP). In presenting the NTHP award, Richard Moe, president of the NTHP, stated that the student housing project was one of the most significant restoration projects in America.

Since the Olympics, the university has continued to work on preserving, rehabilitating, and reusing the remaining buildings. As part of the Olympic Athletes' Village preparations, the university rehabilitated and reused several significant buildings for ancillary uses. These included the former chapel, theater, officer's club, and commander's house. In addition to the buildings restored for the Olympics, the university has put nearly all the available buildings back into active service. Only two buildings in the fort have not been reused since the Olympics, and the university is reprogramming them for future reuse. The post-Olympic restoration has received prestigious accolades as well. The Utah Heritage Foundation, the statewide preservation advocacy organization, recognized the preservation and reuse of the post chapel, post theater, commander's house, and officer's club with individual Preservation Awards in 2002. More recently, the Utah Heritage Foundation (2011) has recognized the university's efforts to rehabilitate a former barracks building into the University of Utah Honors Program Center (2005) and rehabilitating the base commanding officer's house into the Pierre Lassonde Entrepreneur Center (2009) for the David S. Eccles School of Business (fig. 5.2).

Thus, this project demonstrates that careful stewardship can result in the successful large-scale reuse of an underused collection of buildings rather than their wholesale demolition. The positive effects and outcomes from this process have been multifaceted. The athletes of the Olympics were housed in first-class facilities, and the university achieved its goal of expanding and enhancing dormitory space, which in turn has drawn and retained more people on the campus. Beyond those two immediate early goals, the university now has a revitalized residential community and academic foundation on which to continue building its "Living and Learning Community" programs. The buildings themselves demonstrate the ability of policy and decision makers to recognize and fulfill a long-term vision that retains and combines the past,

Figure 5.2. The former post commanding officer's house is now home to the Pierre Lassonde Entrepreneur Center. This rehabilitation won a preservation award from the Utah Heritage Foundation in 2009.

present, and future into a sustainable community. The model that this project provides can be repeated innumerable times as communities seek ways to redevelop underused or vacant former industrial buildings at a broader scale than a single building.

At Fort Douglas, the university's vision for the community of scholars, although spurred by the singular opportunity of the Olympics, provides an example of incrementalism after the Olympics ended. The university did strategically achieve its original short-term goal to improve on-campus dormitory facilities for students, but the longer-term sense of community continues to mature as residential housing services seeks ways to activate the remaining unused buildings and construct or upgrade other facilities nearby. The key element has been the retention of the fort buildings and grounds and its sense of place, which continue to attract growing interest from students and faculty alike.

The most important aspect of this process was to recognize early that completely demolishing the entire fort was virtually impossible due to its National

Historic Landmark status. Additionally, even if the buildings had been de-molished, building anew would have taken far more resources and more money to achieve the level of success that the renovation project has already demonstrated. Furthermore, the recognition that the future long-term incre-mental successes would propel this project further was instrumental in the overall strategy to activate the reuse of the fort. It has not happened overnight, and as with most long-term goals, patience and perseverance are of the utmost importance. The parallel opportunities to revitalize underused neighborhoods of former industrial buildings in a similar manner will continue to grow over the coming decade as policy makers and leaders seek sustainable outcomes in their communities.

Affirming the Environmental Contribution: Christman Company Headquarters, Lansing, Michigan

The Gerding Theater in Portland, Oregon was the first building on the Na-tional Register of Historic Places to earn the LEED Platinum level of recogni-tion (Roberts 2007), and a growing number of historic buildings have joined the various ranks of LEED-rated buildings. One building in particular has dispelled the perception that LEED remains unfriendly to preservation and reuse. The Christman Company Headquarters in Lansing, Michigan (fig. 5.3) has the distinction of being the world's first LEED Triple Platinum build-ing. In 2008, it became the first-ever LEED Double Platinum (for attaining the highest certification in both "Core & Shell" and "Commercial Interiors" categories) building on the National Register of Historic Places. The Christ-man Company's efforts to further green their operations has led to their third LEED Platinum ("Existing Buildings") designation in 2010. The building has also won the prestigious Energy Star Award from the US Environmental Protection Agency (Michigan Municipal League 2010). In doing so, it clearly demonstrates that historic buildings can indeed meet the sustainability goals of contemporary society.

The Christman Company, a construction company founded in 1894, needed additional space for its national headquarters and also wanted to dem-onstrate its commitment to integrated and sustainable design and construc-tion, historic preservation, and the local downtown revitalization. The firm

Figure 5.3. The Christman Building in Lansing, Michigan. (© The
Christman Company. Photo credit: Gene Meadows, used with
permission.)

decided to relocate its headquarters to the heart of Lansing, Michigan's urban
core. In 2006, the firm purchased the 1928 Mutual Building, which had for-
merly housed the headquarters of Michigan Millers Mutual Fire Insurance
Company (Christman Company 2011; Gardi 2011).

The firm specifically selected a previously developed site that included a
landmark building that was functionally obsolete and in disrepair. This tactic
offered an excellent opportunity to show how green historic preservation does
not have to cost more than conventional design and construction practices.
The net project cost after the tax credits was $8.7 million, which included
the "total renovation and upgrade of a historic, but functionally obsolete and

vacant building into a Class A headquarters building" (Gardi 2011: 19). However, the project would not have been done without the economic incentives that were available through a variety of resources, because the extra cost for rehabilitating the building would have reduced the economic attractiveness compared with other properties being considered. Like many preservation and reuse projects, this project required collaboration between the parties involved in the planning, design, and construction and included a public–private partnership agreement with the City of Lansing. The City of Lansing created a development agreement that enabled the project to recapture Michigan Single Business Tax Credits. The city also provided key information to support the application for New Market Tax Credits (NMTCs). The economic incentives that supported this project were as follows:

- $672,500 in State of Michigan Brownfield Single Business Tax Credits
- $2 million in Federal Historic Tax Credits
- $500,000 in State Historic Tax Credits
- Allocation of $8.5 million in NMTCs
- $1.2 million in property tax relief through the Federal Obsolete Property Rehabilitation Act (Christman Company 2011)

The project followed the typical sequence of activities—predesign, design, and construction—but expanded the scope of the sequence to include operations, commissioning, and postoccupancy monitoring not only to ensure that the building systems (e.g., heating, ventilation, and air conditioning [HVAC] equipment and lighting controls) worked properly but also to keep the building systems tuned to the operations of the building.

During the predesign phase, the company conducted a study to develop the design criteria that best represented their core values, people, energy, expertise, accomplishments, and history. The project team included the company's preservation, sustainable design and construction, urban revitalization, real estate development, LEED, and project planning experts, who worked closely with the consulting designers.

Part of the design intent was to create a work environment that increased opportunities for collaboration and interaction between the employees. This resulted in an open office plan that could be readily reconfigured as project workloads shifted over time. This also led to the decision to design a skylit atrium between the two rear extensions of this U-shaped building (fig. 5.4). To preserve the overall exterior appearance of the building, this atrium was not visible from the street.

Because this was a tax credit project, there was a diligent effort during the design phase to meet the *Secretary of the Interior's Standards*. The State

Figure 5.4. The atrium at the Christman Building. (© The Christman Company. Photo credit: Gene Meadows, used with permission.)

Historic Preservation Office and the National Park Service reviewed all design and construction work that affected the character-defining features to ensure that it met the standards protecting the building. The construction included carefully restoring the exterior, main stairway, main corridor, and first floor paneled offices of the five-story limestone and red brick office building. The building's original front façade window frames were meticulously restored and fitted with double-glazed panes to increase their energy efficiency. The building's side and rear exterior windows were replaced with high-efficiency aluminum windows.

The operating, commissioning, and monitoring phases allow for a period to gain greater understanding of how the building works and what it takes to keep operations running smoothly. Preliminary energy modeling for this building showed that the building will lower energy use to 34 percent below minimum energy performance requirements. The HVAC systems minimize energy use while providing individual comfort control. Commissioning on all HVAC, lighting, and domestic water systems ensured that all systems operated as designed. Good indoor air quality is maintained by the air filtration system, reduced use of recirculated air, and carbon dioxide monitoring. The computerized building management system fine-tunes the operation of HVAC and lighting systems. High-efficiency lighting fixtures and T-5 fluorescent lamps provide additional ambient light. All carpeting, paints, coatings, adhesives, and sealants meet rigorous low-emission volatile organic compound (VOC) standards. All office furniture is ergonomic and meets strict VOC standards. Paper, plastic, cardboard, glass, batteries, lamps, and metals are all recycled. The firm also developed an extensive green housekeeping program to further reduce the use of unwanted chemical cleaning products and maintenance practices.

In particular, the accomplishments of the Christman project's design and reuse strategies are as follows:

- This historic building reused embodied energy and existing built resources, helped mitigate suburban sprawl, and enhanced the downtown revitalization efforts.
- The location fosters the use of existing public transportation and parking facilities.
- The design reused 92 percent of existing walls, roof and floors, and most of the company's former office furnishings.

- Extensive recycling diverted 77 percent of construction debris from the landfill.
- Energy use has been reduced by task lighting, occupancy sensors, programmable timers in common areas, daylighting, high-efficiency windows and Energy Star office equipment and appliances.
- Large windows provide views to the outside for 90 percent of the occupants in commercial interior space and daylighting to 92 percent of occupied spaces building-wide.
- The white roof reduces heat island effects.
- Expected energy consumption savings will reduce carbon dioxide emissions by 1,002,945 lb/year, sulfur dioxide emissions by 4,524 gm/year, and nitrogen oxide emissions by 2,148 gm/year, which is equivalent to planting 4,112 trees or driving 1,094,212 fewer miles.
- Renewable Energy Certificates for wind energy offset 70 percent of the building's core and shell electricity use for 2 years and 100 percent of the Christman Company headquarters' electricity use for 2 years. The 843,215-kWh offset reduces carbon dioxide emissions by 1,149,302 lb/year, or the equivalent to planting 5,730 trees or driving 1,254,649 fewer miles.
- High-efficiency HVAC systems provide individually controlled comfort conditions. The under-floor air distribution system maximizes efficient, healthful ventilation.
- Showers and locker rooms encourage walking and bicycling to work.
- Low-flow fixtures reduce water consumption by 40 percent.

The Christman Company reports that they learned the following lessons from the project: Sustainable design and construction does not have to cost more than conventional practices; collaboration between the owner, project team, and subcontractors was essential to success; and the historic preservation and sustainable construction goals of the project were generally complementary (Christman Company 2011).

This project clearly demonstrates that preserving and reusing an existing building can help meet sustainability goals and be economically viable. The Christman Company's expertise in the processes needed to achieve LEED designation, obtain tax credits, and creatively collaborate with city, state, and federal agencies clearly helped them blaze a trail for the recognition of the environmental benefits that stewardship can provide. As more projects like this succeed and gain media attention, they provide increased incentive for others in the industry to become familiar with the economic incentives and processes for building reuse and preservation.

Creating an Economic Catalyst: The Old Post Office, St. Louis, Missouri

The most fundamental parameters for determining success in modern society are the benefits and costs associated with a project and whether they produce positive or negative economic impacts on the investors and community at large. Few projects proceed without some degree of assurance that the outcome will increase economic vibrancy. In the contemporary economic climate, project development processes have become increasingly complex but not necessarily impossible As noted in chapter 4, preservation and reuse can create an economic engine that can transform a neighborhood, district, or community. When well coordinated with various oversight agencies and government economic incentive programs, projects can be a catalyst for substantial improvement of the buildings around them. The following example, the preservation and reuse of the Old Post Office in St. Louis, Missouri (fig. 5.5), shows how a single successful project has prompted a major revitalization effort in an economically distressed portion of the city.

The original construction of the 242,000-square-foot Custom House and Post Office (now known as the Old Post Office) began in 1872 and was completed in 1884 at a cost of approximately $6 million. The Old Post Office is four stories tall with two additional levels below ground. The building occupies a full block in downtown St. Louis. Its monumental proportions make it a major landmark. Of the five Second Empire–style custom houses and post offices built in Boston, Philadelphia, New York, Cincinnati, and St. Louis from 1880 through 1885, the St. Louis Custom House and Post Office is the only one remaining today. The only other major Second Empire–style government building remaining from this period is the State, War and Navy Building in Washington, DC (NTCIC 2011; GlassSteelandStone.com 2011).

Before selling it to the State of Missouri in 2008, the General Services Administration (GSA) had ranked the Old Post Office as the sixth most historic and the seventh most architecturally significant building in its inventory of

Figure 5.5. The Old Post Office Building in Saint Louis, Missouri. (Photo credit: Mark Groth, used with permission.)

more than 2,200 structures. The primary architect was Alfred B. Mullett, who designed many significant state and federal buildings in the late 1800s. The building is important for three reasons: It is an excellent example of the Second Empire style, its original construction details well represent cutting-edge late nineteenth-century technologies; and it represents the vanishing type of federal architecture in a substantial state of preservation and reuse (GlassSteel andStone.com 2011; NTCIC 2011).

The Old Post Office has suffered significant cycles of decline and has twice undergone extensive rehabilitation. The building was initially declared surplus property by the federal government in 1957. Despite preservationists' efforts to save it from demolition in the 1960s and 1970s, the building was vacant by 1975 when the last tenant, a postal substation, moved out. Fortunately, the 1976 Public Building Cooperative Use Act permitted revenue-producing activities to take place in federal buildings and paved the way for adaptive reuse possibilities in GSA facilities nationwide. In January 1976, the GSA published a "Preliminary Feasibility Study for Restoration of U.S. Custom House (Old Post Office), St. Louis, Missouri" (GlassSteelandStone.com 2011) to determine whether the building could be preserved and reused to facilitate new functions. In 1979, the GSA published a Historic Structures Report that verified the historical significance and integrity of its design, construction, and modifications. Between 1978 and 1982, the U.S. GSA completed a $16 million rehabilitation that converted the building into a mixed-use facility shared by federal offices and private commercial establishments. Unfortunately, the rehabilitation did not have the intended economic impact on the local community. Various retail operations tried to make the location work and failed. The building again was vacated and declared surplus in the 1990s.

In late 2000, DESCO Group and DFC Group initiated a redevelopment and financing plan for the building. A review of this project in 2003 led the GSA, the Advisory Council on Historic Preservation, the Missouri State Historic Preservation Office, the Missouri Finance Development Board, the City of St. Louis, and the National Trust for Historic Preservation to sign a programmatic agreement that subsequently produced a $44 million rehabilitation that was completed in 2005. In an environment with greater motivation and awareness of what preservation and reuse can bring and the increased availability of economic incentives, this time the rehabilitation had a significantly different and more positive outcome that has helped to stabilize and revive the surrounding neighborhood (Courts.mo.gov 2011; NTCIC 2011; GlassSteel andStone.com 2011).

The Old Post Office building was fully leased at the time of its 2006 re-dedication. Tenants included the Missouri Court of Appeals, Eastern District, which occupied the entire third and fourth floors; Webster University, which occupied all of the first level below ground with a small administrative office on the street level; and the St. Louis Business Journal, St. Louis Public Library, FOCUS St. Louis, Missouri Attorney General, Missouri Secretary of State, Teach for America, Missouri Department of Health and Senior Services, and Missouri Arts Council, which occupied the remainder of the building (NTCIC 2011; St. Louis' US Custom House & Post Office Building Associates, LLP 2011).

The building is in a qualified low-income community. The site is within a local redevelopment district and qualifies as an additionally distressed area, as defined by the Community Development Financial Institutions Fund. The NTCIC used $22.5 million in NMTCs to enhance an equity investment for the rehabilitation of the Old Post Office building. As a National Historic Landmark, the rehabilitation project was eligible for nearly $7.5 million in federal Historic Tax Credits (HTCs) and nearly $8 million in Missouri HTCs but had to conform to the *Secretary of the Interior's Standards* to qualify. Without this additional equity from the NMTC, the project would not have gone forward, and the Old Post Office, scheduled to be vacated by the GSA, would have been threatened with another cycle of decline or perhaps demolition. As a result of the tax credits, the project instead has less debt and smaller debt service payments, which are a significant incentive to lessen the risks associated with preserving and reusing a historic property in a low-income community (NTCIC 2011).

Overall the preservation and reuse of the Old Post Office has had a palpable impact in the business district around it. The low-income community has benefited from the rehabilitation of the Old Post Office through new businesses, jobs, and students using local business services. The commitment to redevelop the Old Post Office and the subsequent $32.8 million development of the 9th Street Garage has spurred the rehabilitation of numerous adjacent historic properties. Nearby historic property owners stated that they would not have undertaken substantial property improvements had they not been convinced that the Old Post Office project would successfully move forward. Tom Reeves, then the executive director of Downtown NOW!, stated that "the rehabilitation of the Old Post Office was an essential factor in stabilizing the area and catalyzing the rehabilitation of those 10 buildings" (NTCIC 2011).

The economic activity associated directly with the Old Post Office project combined with the leveraged economic activity as a result of the project can be recapped as follows:

- 11 vacant or underused historic buildings rehabilitated
- 1,920,500 rehabbed square feet
- $432.3 million in rehabilitation and development costs
- 576 apartments and condos
- 391,200 square feet of office and retail space
- 89,800 square feet of public library, court, and university space
- 262 new hotel rooms

• A public plaza, historic theater, and two entertainment and conference facilities (NTCIC 2011)

The additional activity that the Old Post Office project has prompted clearly demonstrates the catalytic quality that completing just one well-planned rehabilitation project can create and the importance of the tax incentive programs. The area around the project has witnessed a major boost in economic activity because of the construction itself and the new businesses in the neighborhood. However, this growth has been incremental and organic, expanding block by block through the existing community.

Lessons Learned

Stewardship of the built environment, as described in these case studies and throughout the book, is a viable strategy for increasing sustainability in social, environmental, and economic terms. In many instances, the desired revitalization is a long-term incremental process that may be spurred on through the preservation and reuse of a single building or a group of buildings in a single neighborhood or district. In either scenario, the key element for future success is to recognize that sustainability is the integral and balanced combination of social, environmental, and economic forces.

As the case studies show, the effort to preserve and reuse the largest buildings can be a complex relationship of collaborative practice, public–private partnerships, and interagency agreements, and although such projects are complex, they are not impossible. For small residential projects such as the reuse of a family home, these relationships and processes also exist, but they are generally simpler because of the reduced scale and scope of work.

The financing and other incentive programs available for preservation, reuse, and sustainability indicate that the government has a strong interest in conserving existing social, environmental, and economic resources while revitalizing buildings, neighborhoods, and communities. Through changes in laws that previously favored new construction, government also recognizes the value of keeping buildings intact and out of the landfill. Acceptance of preservation and reuse as the ultimate form of recycling will reduce pressures for further extraction and depletion of natural resources for new building materials and reduce demolition waste pressures on landfills.

There is also a growing awareness that the land use policies of the mid- to late twentieth century often precluded the preservation or reuse of the built environment, promoted increased use of nonrenewable energy sources, and imposed increased social, environmental, and infrastructural costs that are inherently not sustainable. As we adapt to living on a planet with increasingly scarce resources, we must begin to value land use that improves ecological performance through strategies that complement the sustainability of a building or site at the local and regional level. The challenge will be in establishing this as more common practice rather than an innovative exception to business as usual.

Future Directions and Imperatives

To increase the prevalence of preservation and reuse in development projects, it is necessary to foster the greater realization of the broad advantages of these types of projects. Policies and incentives that encourage preservation and reuse over new construction are needed. Along with dispelling the many myths, misperceptions, and biases surrounding preservation and reuse, advocates must continue to develop the collaborative processes and networks that enable them to gain an effective voice in this forum. A crucial aspect of involvement is for those who understand the advantages of preservation and reuse to help policy and decision makers at all levels and in all market sectors understand how the stewardship ethic of preserving and reusing buildings fits into the overall schema of sustainable design trends.

Advocates must continue to be proactive in anticipating how the market perceives and accepts this conservation approach to the built environment. Some encouraging sustainability trends appear to be increasing interest in preservation and reuse.

Although many green building trends are observed in practices geared toward new construction, these practices can be extended to opportunities that are similarly available in preserving and reusing buildings. The key is, as Marcel Proust notes, to have "new eyes." For example, the green building trends that the Earth Advantage Institute has defined for 2011 (Earth Advantage Institute 2011) can be extended to existing buildings as noted here:

- *Affordable green.* Continued evolution and growth of this market sector is making high-performance, healthy new homes more affordable. In the existing home market, energy upgrades are now available through programs that include low-cost audits and utility bill–based financing to enable homeowners to take advantage of them.
- *Sharing and comparing home energy use.* A growing number of tools are available to track your home energy usage, including the website Earth Aid, which lets users track home energy usage, earn rewards for energy savings from local vendors, and compare their home energy consumption with others'. This opportunity will help homeowners in historic and older buildings compare what may work best for their home or neighborhood.
- *Outcome-based energy code (OBEC).* Prescriptive energy codes used in commercial remodels do not encourage effective retrofitting. OBECs will provide the flexibility and latitude to make retrofits a more attractive option. The City of Seattle, the New Building Institute, and the NTHP's Preservation Green Lab are working together to develop such a code for new and existing buildings. Code officials must be able to interpret the code to accommodate the conditions commonly found in historic and older buildings.
- *Community purchasing power.* Neighborhoods will join together to obtain better pricing on green technology purchases and installation costs. This is particularly advantageous for historic residential districts, because the economy of scale in purchasing will allow greater price discounting when a vendor or supplier can count on a larger volume of sales than would occur with single-home purchases.
- *Intersection of smart homes, grid-aware appliances, and smart grid.* These appliances include sophisticated energy management capabilities to enable homeowners to monitor their electricity usage and increase or decrease usage by remote control. Just because a building is historic or old does not mean it is incompatible with cutting-edge technology that can use programmable timers, Internet access, and digital telephone applications to reduce energy and water use.

- *Accessory dwelling units.* These small independent units are the ideal for energy savings and sustainable construction. Detached or attached, they help cities increase urban density and restrict sprawl and permit homeowners to increase their property value. Portland, Oregon and Santa Cruz, California have waived administrative fees to encourage the creation of accessory dwelling units that increase urban density and mitigate sprawl. The social diversity of a community will increase with the range of tenants typically seeking these types of living quarters.

- *Rethinking of residential heating and cooling.* Builders and homeowners will continue to become more mindful of higher-performance materials and construction practices, such as those described in the increasingly popular "Passive House" standard originally developed in Europe. This will also include using smaller but more efficient furnaces and air conditioners, and ground-coupled (i.e., geothermal) heat pumps will also continue to climb in popularity. As the cost of heating and cooling a home decreases, the more affordable living (and remaining) in a neighborhood becomes.

- *Residential graywater use.* Based on known and projected water shortages in many areas, particularly in the American southwest and California, the demand for recycling graywater is growing. Graywater systems divert water that contains no human waste to other uses such as lawn irrigation and groundwater, reducing overall water use and demands on septic and stormwater systems. Here again, the introduction of cost and resource use reduction measures promotes social and environmental stability in a community.

- *Small commercial certification.* To encourage smaller commercial projects (less than 50,000 sf) to go green, alternative certification programs have emerged. These include Earthcraft Light Commercial and Earth Advantage Commercial. Many of the associated costs of certification programs such as LEED are viewed as prohibitively expensive for small building owners and developers. These smaller commercial enterprises occur in much of the existing historic and older building stock that is readily available and often underused.

- *Life cycle analysis (LCA).* LCA examines the impact of materials over their lifetime through environmental indicators such as embodied energy, solid waste, air and water pollution, and global warming potential.

This process will enable architects to determine what the avoided impacts are for each design strategy they are considering. Early use of this analysis has already indicated that preserving and reusing buildings may be far more sustainable practice than previously understood.

The strategy of preserving and reusing buildings, when extended to social, environmental, and economic sustainability and the recognition of the stewardship synergies that it can provide, is a powerful tool that can increase opportunities to accomplish the goals of sustainability in the twenty-first century and beyond. As noted by NTHP president Richard Moe in his opening report to the 2007 National Preservation Conference,

> Now, we're on the threshold of a new phase as growing numbers of people are concerned about the degradation of the environment and our relentless consumption of irreplaceable energy and natural resources. Preservation certainly isn't the solution to these problems, but it can be—and should be—an important part of the solution. (Moe 2007)

This statement promotes the use of preservation as part of the sustainability strategies inherent in stewardship of the built environment. As successful projects increasingly dispel the common misperceptions and myths about preservation and the reuse of buildings, this approach to stewardship can continue to play an integral, and increasing, role in local and global sustainability.

Property values, job creation, and tax revenues are important economic indicators that describe how well an area is doing economically, but it is the vitality and sense of community that is often the measure people value, relate to most directly, and consider to be a significant part of their overall life satisfaction. Whether expressed as social equity, environmental synergies, or economic growth, communities that balance the social, environmental, and economic factors discussed throughout this book are the ones that are likely to offer a higher quality of life.

Unfortunately, the risk-averse nature of most participants in the planning, design, engineering, construction, operations, and asset management aspects of buildings inhibits acceptance of the broader reach provided by stewardship of the built environment through preserving and reusing existing buildings.

Although there are encouraging trends, such as those detailed in the previous list, there are still many challenges for the preservation and reuse markets. These challenges include getting a broader spectrum of people to

- See preserving and reusing buildings as affordable, sustainable, and capable of meeting contemporary and future demands of twenty-first century living. Along with lifestyle choices for increasing population density, policies and programs that incentivize and promote sustainable building products and processes need to be developed and funded.
- Recognize and support the implementation of district energy systems and the broader use of ecodistricts to gain an economy of scale in purchasing power for sustainability enhancements at the neighborhood scale. This has significant opportunities for use in historic districts or communities whose oversight guidelines may restrict or prohibit the use of solar panels and photovoltaic panels in locations viewable from a public way.
- Develop strategies that reduce demand for water and minimize waste. There is a growing awareness that issues concerning the supply and demand for water will eventually surpass current discussions on energy efficiency.
- Meet the growing demand for information, in part by using social media and information-based sharing sites and programs, as well as seeking better ways to identify, monitor, and evaluate progress on energy and water use reduction goals.
- Support publication of project outcomes (both positive and negative) that need to be brought to the attention of the spectrum of decision makers and policy shapers who mediate building preservation and reuse policies, such as municipal, state, and federal elected officials, local and state review boards, and professional societies serving the building planning, design, construction, and operation service industries.
- Foster the shift toward LCA tools that describe the avoided impacts of project choices. Because this tool tends to favor projects that reduce sprawl and the attendant effects of automobile usage, the emerging recognition of the sustainability value of building preservation and reuse will become more readily apparent.
- Continue the movement away from prescriptive codes and performance standards that are based primarily on the new construction practices.

Outcome-based codes and smart codes are the first step in this direction, but work on these policies needs to continue and expand.

Whereas looking solely at new construction to achieve sustainability goals perpetuates the extraction and depletion mode of thinking that got society where it is today, the use of stewardship of the built environment will expand perspectives on how to fully engage and truly achieve a sustainable environment. As the numerous examples of successful preservation and reuse projects show, it is more possible than ever to achieve sustainability through the social, environmental, and economic gains that stewardship of the built environment provides. There are strong indications that preservation and reuse has increasing potential to significantly contribute to a sustainable future: the growing interest in places that engage people with connections to their heritage, the recognition of the environmental benefits that preserving and reusing buildings has on finite resources, and the development of a variety of funding mechanisms and incentives to reduce risk-averse development to undertake these projects. Stewardship of the built environment, with its focus on the preservation and reuse of buildings, is a viable alternate approach to new construction—however green the new building might be—offering a combined land use, environmental conservation, and economic growth strategy to build denser, more attractive urban places that foster greater sustainability in both the built and the natural environments.

Abbreviations

ACHP	Advisory Council on Historic Preservation
ADA	Americans with Disabilities Act
AIA	American Institute of Architects
ANHA	Association of National Heritage Areas
ANSI	American National Standards Institute
APT	Association for Preservation Technology
ASHRAE	American Society of Heating, Refrigerating and Air-Conditioning Engineers
ASMI	Athena Sustainable Materials Institute
BREEAM	Building Research Establishment Environmental Assessment Method
C&D	Construction and demolition
CDBG	Community Development Block Grant
CDE	Community Development Entity
CDFI	Community Development Financial Institutions
CLG	Certified Local Government
EECBG	Energy Efficiency and Conservation Block Grant
EPA	Environmental Protection Agency
EPACT	Environmental Policy Act
EUI	Energy utilization index
FAR	Floor area ratio
GSA	General Services Administration
HABS	Historic American Buildings Survey
HPF	Historic Preservation Fund
HTC	Historic Tax Credit
HUD	US Department of Housing and Urban Development
HVAC	Heating, ventilation, and air conditioning
IAQ	Indoor air quality
IBC	International Building Code
ICCROM	International Centre for the Study of the Preservation and Restoration of Cultural Property
IEBC	International Existing Building Code
IESNA	Illuminating Engineering Society of North America

IGCC	International Green Construction Code
ILSR	Institute for Local Self-Reliance
INTBAU	International Network for Traditional Building, Architecture & Urbanism
IRS	Internal Revenue Service
LCA	Life cycle analysis
LEED	Leadership in Energy and Environmental Design
LIC	Low-income community
LIHTC	Low-Income Housing Tax Credit
LODO	Lower Downtown (Denver)
MEP	Mechanical, electrical, and plumbing
NASA	National Aeronautics and Space Administration
NCSHPO	National Conference of State Historic Preservation Officers
NDT	Nondestructive testing
NECPA	National Energy Conservation Policy Act
NEPA	National Environmental Policy Act
NHPA	National Historic Preservation Act
NMSC	National Main Street Center
NMTC	New Market Tax Credit
NPS	National Park Service
NREL	National Renewable Energy Laboratory
NRHP	National Register of Historic Places
NTCIC	National Trust Community Investment Corporation
NTHP	National Trust for Historic Preservation
OECD	Office of Economic and Community Development
OPEC	Organization of the Petroleum Exporting Countries
PGL	Preservation Green Lab
PPP	People–planet–profit
QRE	Qualified rehabilitation expenditure
RDA	Redevelopment Authority
SAT	Save America's Treasures
SBE	Stewardship of the built environment
SD	Sustainable design
SDL	Simulated divided lite
SEE	Social–environmental–economic
SHPO	State historic preservation office
Soho	South of Houston Street (New York)
TDR	Transfer of development rights
TIF	Tax increment financing
Tribeca	Triangle Below Canal (New York)
TDL	True divided lite

UNESCO   United Nations Educational, Scientific and Cultural Organization
USDOE   United States Department of Energy
USEPA   United States Environmental Protection Agency
USGBC   United States Green Building Council
VMT   Vehicle miles traveled
WBDG   Whole Building Design Guide
WCED   World Commission on Environment and Development

Recommendations for Further Reading

This appendix includes two sections, "Important Links" and "Recommended Readings," for further exploration beyond the references already cited on topics that will complement or enhance understanding of stewardship of the built environment.

Important Links

Advisory Council on Historic Preservation (ACHP)
http://www.achp.gov/

Association for Preservation Technology (APT)
http://www.apti.org/

Athena Sustainable Materials Institute (ASMI)
http://www.athenasmi.org

EcoCity Builders
http://www.ecocitybuilders.org/about-us/

Institute for Local Self-Reliance (ILSR)
http://www.ilsr.org/

Internal Revenue Service (IRS)
Market Segment Specialization Program (MSSP) Rehabilitation Tax Credit: http://www.irs.gov/pub/irs-mssp/rehab.pdf

International Making Cities Livable Council
http://www.livablecities.org/

National Alliance of Preservation Commissioners (NAPC)

http://www.uga.edu/napc/programs/napc/guidelines.htm

National Conference of State Historic Preservation Officers (NCSHPO)

http://www.ncshpo.org/

National Park Service (NPS)

Accessibility: http://www.nps.gov/history/hps/tps/briefs/brief32.htm

Energy conservation: http://www.nps.gov/history/hps/tps/briefs/brief03.htm

Federal tax credits and incentives: http://www.nps.gov/history/hps/tps/tax/index.htm

Funding for preservation: http://www.nps.gov/history/hps/hpg/downloads/Show
   _Me_the_Money2009.pdf

Heating, ventilating, and cooling historic buildings: http://www.nps.gov/history/hps/
   tps/briefs/brief24.htm

Heritage documentation programs: http://www.nps.gov/hdp/

Historic preservation tax incentives: http://www.nps.gov/history/hps/TPS/tax/

Historic Preservation Tax Incentive Program 2010 annual report: http://www.nps
   .gov/tps/tax-incentives/taxdocs/Federal-Tax-Incentives-2010Annual.pdf

National Register of Historic Places (NRHP): http://www.nps.gov/nr/

Secretary of the Interior's Standards: http://www.nps.gov/tps/standards/rehabilitation/
   rehab/index.htm

Sustainability guidelines: http://www.nps.gov/history/hps/tps/download/guidelines
   -sustainability.pdf

Technical preservation services (includes preservation brief series): http://www.nps
   .gov/tps/

Weatherization: http://www.nps.gov/history/hps/tps/weather/index.html

National Trust for Historic Preservation (NTHP)

National Main Street Center (NMSC): http://www.preservationnation.org/
   main-street/

National Trust Community Investment Corporation: http://www.ntcicfunds.com/

National Trust for Historic Preservation (NTHP): http://www.preservationnation
   .org/

Preservation Green Lab: http://www.preservationnation.org/issues/sustainability/
   green-lab/additional-resources/PGL-2-pager-FINAL.pdf

Weatherization: http://www.preservationnation.org/issues/weatherization/

Windows: http://www.preservationnation.org/about-us/regional-offices/northeast/
additional-resources/2009-Revised-Window-Tip-Sheet-1.pdf

United States Department of Energy (USDOE)
Energy Efficiency and Conservation Block Grant (EECBG) program:
http://www1.eere.energy.gov/wip/eecbg.html

United States Department of Housing and Urban Development (HUD)
Community Development Block Grant Program: http://www.hud.gov/offices/cpd/
communitydevelopment/library/historicpreservation/historicpreservation.doc

United States Department of the Treasury (USTREAS)
American Recovery and Reinvestment Act: http://www.ustreas.gov/recovery/
Community Development Financial Institutions Fund: http://www.cdfifund.gov/
what_we_do/programs_id.asp?programid=5

United States Environmental Protection Agency (EPA)
Resource conservation: http://www.epa.gov/epawaste/conserve/rrr/imr/cdm/index.htm

Whole Building Design Guide (WBDG)
Life safety and security: http://www.wbdg.org/design/accommodate_needs.php
Sustainable preservation: http://www.wbdg.org/resources/sustainable_hp.php

Recommended Reading

Advisory Council on Historic Preservation (ACHP). 1989. *Fire Safety Retrofitting in
Historic Buildings*. Washington, DC: Government Printing Office.
Alderson, Caroline, and Nick Artim. 2000. Fire-safety retrofitting: Innovative
solutions for ornamental building interiors. *APT Bulletin* 31(2/3):26–32.
Allison, Eric, and Lauren Peters. 2011. *Historic Preservation and the Livable City*.
Hoboken, NJ: Wiley.
American Planning Association. 2010. New federal block grants are an opportunity
of U.S. planners. Accessed February 26, 2009, http://postcarboncities.net/
node/2343.
Barnett, Jonathan. 2003. *Redesigning Cities: Principles, Practice, Implementation*.
Chicago: Planners Press.
Barton, Hugh, Marcus Grant, and Richard Guise. 2003. *Shaping Neighborhoods: A
Guide for Health, Sustainability, and Vitality*. London: Spon Press.

Beasley, Ellen. 1998. *Design and Development: Infill Compatible with Historic Neighborhoods*. Washington, DC: National Trust for Historic Preservation.

Benfield, F. Kaid, Matthew D. Raimi, and Donald D. T. Chen. 1999. *Once There Were Greenfields: How Urban Sprawl Is Undermining America's Environment, Economy, and Social Fabric*. Washington, DC: National Resources Defense Council.

Benfield, F. Kaid, Jutka Terris, and Nancy Vorsanger. 2001. *Solving Sprawl: Models of Smart Growth in Communities across America*. Washington, DC: National Resources Defense Council.

Breen, Ann, and Dick Rigby. 2004. *Intown Living: A Different American Dream*. Washington, DC: Island Press.

Brookings Institution Center on Metropolitan Policy. 2003. *Back to Prosperity: A Competitive Agenda for Renewing Pennsylvania*. Washington, DC: The Brookings Institution. http://www.brookings.edu/es/urban/pa/chapter1.pdf.

Brown, Lance Jay, David Dixon, and Oliver Gillham. 2009. *Urban Design for an Urban Century*. Hoboken, NJ: Wiley.

Brown, Marilyn A., Frank Southworth, and Andrea Sarzynski. 2008. *Shrinking the Carbon Footprint of Metropolitan America*. Washington, DC: The Brookings Institution. Accessed June 18, 2010, http://www.brookings.edu/~/media/Files/rc/reports/2008/05_carbon_footprint_sarzynski/carbonfootprint_report.pdf.

Carroon, Jeanne, Allen Roberts, and Soren Simonsen. 2004. "Green" design and historic buildings. *Forum News* X(3):1–2, 6.

Carter, Calvin W. 1981. Assessing energy conservation benefits: A study. In *New Energy from Old Buildings*, 103–11. Washington, DC: National Trust for Historic Preservation.

Cascadia Consulting Group. 2006. Targeted Statewide Waste Characterization Study. Detailed characterization for construction and demolition waste. California Integrated Waste Management Board. Accessed June 28, 2010, http://www.calrecycle.ca.gov/publications/Disposal/34106007.pdf.

Cascadia Consulting Group, DSM Environmental Services, MSW Consultants. 2007. Delaware Solid Waste Authority statewide waste characterization study, 2006–07. Final report. Accessed June 28, 2010, http://www.dswa.com/pdfs/reports/Statewide%20Waste%20Characterization%20Study%202006-2007.pdf.

Cassar, May. 2009. Sustainable heritage: Challenges and strategies for the twenty-first century. *APT Bulletin* 40(1):3–11.

Cavallo, James. 2005. Capturing energy-efficiency opportunities in historic houses. *APT Bulletin* 36(4):19–23.

Cazayoux, Edward Jon. 2003. *A Manual for the Environmental and Climatic Responsive Restoration and Renovation of Older Houses in Louisiana*. Baton Rouge: Louisiana Department of Natural Resources.

Cole, Raymond. 1996. Life-cycle energy use in office buildings. *Buildings and Environment* 31(4):307–17.

Connolly, William M. 2003. The New Jersey Rehabilitation Subcode and historic preservation. *APT Bulletin* 34(4):19–21.

Cooper, Joyce Smith. 2003. Life-cycle assessment and sustainable development indicators. *Journal of Industrial Ecology* 7(1):12–15.

Cox, Rachel S. 2001. *Controlling Disaster: Earthquake-Hazard Reduction for Historic Buildings.* Washington, DC: National Trust for Historic Preservation.

———. 2002. *Design Review in Historic Districts.* Washington, DC: National Trust for Historic Preservation.

Crankshaw, Neil. 2009. *Creating Vibrant Public Spaces: Streetscape Design in Commercial and Historic Districts.* Washington, DC: Island Press.

Cunningham, Storm. 2002. *The Restoration Economy: The Greatest New Growth Frontier.* San Francisco, CA: Berrett-Koehler.

Dono, Andrea, ed. 2009. *Revitalizing Main Street: A Practitioner's Guide to Comprehensive Commercial District Revitalization.* Washington, DC: National Trust for Historic Preservation.

Dowling, Joanna. 2009. Blanketing the home: The use of thermal insulation in American housing, 1920–1945. *APT Bulletin* 40(1):33–39.

DSM Environmental Services. 2002. *Vermont Waste Composition Study.* Vermont Department of Environmental Conservation, June 2002. Accessed June 28, 2010, http://www.anr.state.vt.us/dec/wastediv/solid/pubs/VT%20WASTE%20COMP .pdf.

Dunham-Jones, Ellen, and June Williamson. 2009. *Retrofitting Suburbia: Urban Design Solutions for Redesigning Suburbs.* Hoboken, NJ: Wiley.

Elefante, Carl. 2005. Historic preservation and sustainable development: Lots to learn, lots to teach. *APT Bulletin* 36(4):53.

Ewing, Reid, Keith Bartholomew, Steve Winkelman, Jerry Walters, and Don Chen. 2008. *Growing Cooler: Evidence on Urban Development and Climate Change Executive Summary.* Washington, DC: The Urban Land Institute. Accessed October 21, 2009, http://www.1kfriends.org/documents/Growing_Cooler _Executive_Summary.pdf.

Farr, Douglas. 2008. *Sustainable Urbanism: Urban Design with Nature.* Hoboken, NJ: Wiley.

Fisher, Charles E., and Hugh C. Miller, eds. 1998. *Caring for Your Historic House: Preserving and Maintaining Structural Systems, Roofs, Masonry, Plaster, Wallpapers, Paint, Mechanical and Electrical Systems, Windows, Woodwork, Flooring, Landscapes.* New York: Henry N. Abrams.

Fitch, James Marston, and William Bobenhausen. 1999. *American Building: The Environmental Forces That Shape It*. New York: Oxford University Press.

Florida, Richard. 2002. *The Rise of the Creative Class*. New York: Basic Books.

Ford, Larry R. 2003. *Revitalization or Reinvention? America's New Downtowns*. Baltimore, MD: The Johns Hopkins University Press.

Foster, Margaret. 2008. Block of historic downtown Lexington may be leveled for "green" hotel. *Preservation Magazine*, April 16, 2008. Accessed June 18, 2010, http://www.preservationnation.org/magazine/2008/todays-news/block-of -historicdowntown-lex.html.

Friedman, Donald. 2000. *The Investigation of Buildings: A Guide for Architects, Engineers, and Owners*. New York: W.W. Norton.

Frumkin, Howard, Lawrence Frank, and Richard Jackson. 2004. *Urban Sprawl and Public Health: Designing, Planning, and Building for Healthy Communities*. Washington, DC: Island Press.

Gale, Francis, ed. 2008. *Preservation Technology Primer*. Springfield, IL: Association for Preservation Technology.

Glisson, Linda. 2000. *Revitalizing Downtown: The Professional's Guide to the Main Street Approach*. Washington, DC: National Trust Main Street Center.

Gratz, Roberta B. 1994. *The Living City: How America's Cities Are Being Revitalized by Thinking Big in a Small Way*. New York: Wiley.

Gratz, Roberta B., and N. Mintz. 1998. *Cities Back from the Edge: New Life for Downtown*. New York: Wiley.

Green, Melvyn, and Anne L. Watson. 2005. *Building Codes and Historic Buildings*. Washington, DC: National Trust for Historic Preservation.

Grogan, Paul S., and Tony Proscio. 2000. *Comeback Cities: A Blueprint for Urban Neighborhood Revival*. Boulder, CO: Westview.

Gutfreund, Owen D. 2004. *Twentieth-Century Sprawl: Highways and the Reshaping of the American Landscape*. New York: Oxford University Press.

Harris, Samuel Y. 2001. *Building Pathology: Deterioration, Diagnostics, and Intervention*. New York: Wiley.

Hayden, Delores. 2003. *Building Suburbia: Green Fields and Urban Growth 1820– 2000*. New York: Pantheon.

Henry, Michael C. 2007. From the outside in: Preventive conservation, sustainability, and environmental management. *Getty Conservation Institute Newsletter* 22:1. Accessed June 28, 2010, http://www.getty.edu/conservation/ publications/newsletters/22_1/feature.html.

Hirschhorn, Joel S. 2005. *Sprawl Kills: How Blandburbs Steal Your Time, Health and Money*. New York: Sterling & Ross.

Hudnut, William H. 2003. *Halfway to Everywhere: A Portrait of America's First-Tier Suburbs*. Washington, DC: Urban Land Institute.

Insall, Donald. 2008. *Living Buildings*. Mulgrave, Victoria, AUS: Image Publishing Group.

International Code Council. 2006. *International Existing Building Code 2006*. Falls Church, VA: International Code Council.

———. 2009. *International Energy Conservation Code*. Country Club Hills, IL: International Code Council.

Jackson, Mike. 2003. Main street and building codes: The "tin ceiling" challenge. *APT Bulletin* 34(4):29–34.

———. 2005. Building a culture that sustains design. *APT Bulletin* 36(4):2.

Jacobs, Jane. 1985. *Cities and the Wealth of Nations: Principles of Economic Life*. New York: Vintage Books.

———. 1992. *The Death and Life of Great American Cities*. New York: Vintage.

Johnson, Elizabeth. 1997. *The Thoreau Center for Sustainability: A Model Public–Private Partnership*. Washington, DC: National Trust for Historic Preservation.

Kaplan, Marilyn. 2003a. Considering fire-safety improvements in historic buildings. *APT Bulletin* 34(4):10–17.

———. 2003b. Rehabilitation codes come of age: A search for alternative approaches. *APT Bulletin* 34(4):5–8.

———. 2007. Adopting 21st century codes for historic buildings. *Model Public Policies* (A Public Policy Report published by National Trust Forum) (May/June):1–8.

Kibert, Charles J. 2005. *Sustainable Construction: Green Building Design and Delivery*. New York: Wiley.

Klunder, Laura, and Glenda Itard. 2007. Comparing environmental impacts of renovated housing stock with new construction. *Building Research & Information* 35(3):252–67.

Kotkin, Joel. 2000. *The New Geography: How the Digital Revolution Is Reshaping the American Landscape*. New York: Random House.

Kromer, John. 2010. *Fixing Broken Cities: The Implementation of Urban Development Strategies*. New York: Routledge.

Lally, Patrick. 2005. Community Restoration and Revitalization Act: Improving the rehab tax credit. *Forum News* XI(4)(March/April):1–2.

Lechner, Norbert. 2008. *Heating Cooling Lighting: Design Methods for Architects*, 3rd ed. Hoboken, NJ: Wiley.

Longstreth, Richard, ed. 2008. *Cultural Landscapes: Balancing Nature and Heritage in Preservation Practice*. Minneapolis: University of Minnesota Press.

Lubeck, Aaron. 2010. *Green Restorations: Sustainable Building and Historic Homes.* Gabriola Island, BC: New Society Publishers.

Lucy, William H., and David Phillips. 2000. *Confronting Suburban Decline: Strategic Planning for Metropolitan Renewal.* Washington, DC: Island Press.

McLure, Frank. 2006. *Modern Earthquake Codes: History and Development.* Berkeley, CA: Computers and Structures. Accessed February 3, 2007, http://www.csiberkeley.com/Tech_Info/McClure_book_smll.pdf.

Mendler, Sandra, William Odell, and Mary Ann Lazarus. 2006. *The HO+K Guidebook to Sustainable Design,* 2nd ed. New York: Wiley.

Merryman, Helena. 2005. Structural materials in historic restoration: Environmental issues and greener strategies. *APT Bulletin* 36(4):31–38.

Miara, Jim. 2004. The New Markets Tax Credit Program: A CEOs for Cities briefing paper: How this new incentive can strengthen America's cities. Accessed July 17, 2010, http://www.cdfa.net/cdfa/cdfaweb.nsf/fbaad5956b2928b086256efa0 05c5f78/62e208369e357303862573ef0057ca9c/$FILE/New_Markets_Tax_Credit _Program.pdf.

Miller, Julia H. 2004. *A Layperson's Guide to Historic Preservation Law: A Survey of Federal, State and Local Laws Governing Historic Resource Protection.* Washington, DC: National Trust for Historic Preservation.

National Trust for Historic Preservation. 1976. *Economic Benefits of Preserving Old Buildings.* Washington, DC: The Preservation Press.

———. 1980. *Old and New Architecture: Design Relationship.* Washington, DC: Preservation Press.

———. 1992. *Reviewing New Construction Projects in Historic Areas.* Washington, DC: National Trust for Historic Preservation.

———. 2002. State funding for historic preservation: A state by state summary. Forum focus supplement in *Forum News* VIII(5)(May/June):1–8.

National Trust Staff. 2002. Historic rehabilitation tax credits: Today and tomorrow. *Forum News* VIII(3)(January/February):1–2, 6.

Oldenburg, Ray. 1999. *The Great Good Place: Cafes, Coffee Shops, Bookstores, Bars, Hair Salons and Other Hangouts at the Heart of a Community.* Philadelphia: DeCapo.

Orr, David W. 2009. *Down to the Wire: Confronting Climate Collapse.* New York: Oxford University Press.

Owen, David. 2009. *Green Metropolis: Why Living Smaller, Living Closer, and Driving Less Are the Keys to Sustainability.* New York: Riverhead.

Pianca, Elizabeth G. 2001. Smart codes: A new approach to building codes. *Forum News* 3(5):1–2, 6.

Porter, Douglas R. 2002. *Making Smart Growth Work*. Washington, DC: Urban Land Institute.

Powter, Andrew, and Susan Ross. 2005. Integrating environmental and cultural sustainability for heritage properties. *APT Bulletin* 36(4):5–11.

Rabun, J. Stanley. 2000. *Structural Analysis of Historic Buildings: Restoration, Preservation and Adaptive Reuse for Architects and Engineers*. New York: Wiley.

Roberts, Tristan. 2007. Historic preservation and green building: A lasting relationship. *Environmental Building News* (January 2007). Accessed June 28, 2010, http://www.preservationnation.org/issues/sustainability/additional -resources/HPandGreenBuildingArticle.pdf.

Rodwell, Dennis. 2007. *Conservation and Sustainability in Historic Cities*. Malden, MA: Blackwell.

Rose, William B. 2006. Should walls of historic buildings be insulated? *APT Bulletin* 36(4):13–18.

Rubman, Kerri. 2004. Promoting rehab tax credits in Baltimore. *Forum News* X(5) (May/June):1–2, 6.

Ruth, Matthias, ed. 2006. *Smart Growth and Climate Change: Regional Development, Infrastructure and Adaptation*. Northampton, MA: Edward Elgar.

Rypkema, Donovan. 2007. *Feasibility Assessment Manual for Reusing Historic Buildings*. Washington, DC: National Trust for Historic Preservation.

———. 2008. Heritage conservation and the local economy. *Global Urban Development* 4(1)(August). Accessed June 5, 2010, http://www.globalurban.org/ GUDMag08Vol4Iss1/Rypkema.htm.

Satow, Julie. 2010. Showing the benefits of "green" retrofits. *The New York Times*, June 1, 2010. Accessed June 7, 2010, http://www.nytimes.com/2010/06/02/ realestate/commercial/02deutsche.html?_r=1&ref=commercial.

Schmickle, Bill. 2007. *The Politics of Historic Districts: A Primer for Grassroots Preservation*. Lanham, MD: Alta Mira.

Scientific Application International Corporation. 2006. *Life Cycle Assessment: Principles and Practice*. Cincinnati, OH: United States Environmental Protection Agency. Accessed June 18, 2010, http://www.epa.gov/nrmrl/lcaccess/ pdfs/600r06060.pdf.

Sedovic, Walter, and Jill H. Gotthelf. 2005. What replacement windows can't replace: The real cost of removing historic windows. *APT Bulletin* 36(4):25–29.

Sewall, Jim, and Claudette Hanks Reischel. 2005. *Treatment of Flood-Damaged Older and Historic Buildings*. Washington, DC: National Trust for Historic Preservation.

Stewart, Erica. 2004. The New Markets Tax Credit: A new financing tool for historic rehab and Main Street projects. *Forum News* X(5)(May/June):3.

Sucher, David. 2003. *City Comforts: How to Build an Urban Village*. Seattle: City
   Comforts Inc.

Talen, Emily. 2005. *New Urbanism and American Planning: The Conflicts of Cultures*.
   New York: Routledge.

Thormark, Catarina. 2002. A low energy building in a life-cycle: Its embodied
   energy, energy need for operation and recycling potential. *Building and
   Environment* 37(4):429–35.

Throsby, David. 2003. Sustainability in the conservation of the built environment:
   An economist's perspective. In *Managing Change: Sustainable Approaches to
   Conservation of the Built Environment,* edited by J. M. Teutonico and F. Matero,
   3–10. Los Angeles: Getty Conservation Institute.

United States Department of Housing and Urban Development. 2000. *Guideline
   on Fire Ratings of Archaic Materials and Assemblies*. Washington, DC: US
   Department of Housing and Urban Development.

Urban Land Institute. 1998. *ULI on the Future: Smart Growth—Economy,
   Community, Environment*. Washington, DC: Urban Land Institute.

———. 1999. *Smart Growth: Myth and Fact™*. Washington, DC: Urban Land
   Institute.

———. 2001. *Urban Infill Housing: Myth and Fact™*. Washington, DC: Urban
   Land Institute.

Van Hoffman, A. 2003. *House by House, Block by Block: The Rebirth of America's
   Urban Neighborhoods*. New York: Oxford University Press.

Wheeler, Stephen M., and Timothy Beatley, eds. 2004. *The Sustainable Urban
   Development Reader*. New York: Routledge.

Winter, Thomas A. 2003. A pioneering effort: The California State Historical
   Building Code. *APT Bulletin* 34(4):17–21.

References

2020 Climate Campaign. 2011. International ecocity standards. Accessed August 9, 2011, http://2020climatecampaign.org/sites/default/files/IES_2pages.pdf.

Adams, Ron. 2005. Atomic Insights: Too cheap to meter—It's now true. Accessed November 27, 2011, http://www.atomicinsights.com/AI_03-09-05.html.

Advisory Council on Historic Preservation (ACHP). 1979a. *Assessing the Energy Conservation Benefits of Historic Preservation: Methods and Examples.* Washington, DC: Advisory Council on Historic Preservation. Accessed on November 27, 2011, http://www.achp.gov/1979%20-%20Energy%20Conserv%20 and%20Hist%20Pres.pdf.

———. 1979b. *Preservation and Energy Conservation.* Washington, DC: Advisory Council on Historic Preservation.

———. 2010. Federal historic preservation case law 1966–1996. Accessed on November 27, 2011, http://www.achp.gov/book/sectionVIII.html.

Affordable Housing Resource Center. 2010. Resources: About LIHTC. Accessed July 16, 2010, http://www.novoco.com/low_income_housing/resources/program _summary.php.

Alliance of National Heritage Areas (ANHA). 2006. Economic impact of heritage tourism spending 2005. Accessed July 26, 2010, http://72.41.119.75/Library/ Tourism/ANHA_Heritage_Eco_Imp_Report.pdf.

Athena Sustainable Materials Institute (ASMI). 2009. A life cycle assessment study of embodied effects for existing historic buildings. Accessed November 25, 2011, http://www.athenasmi.org/publications/docs/Athena_LCA_for_Existing_Historic _Buildings.pdf.

———. 2011. Case studies: The Edge Office Building. Accessed November 25, 2011, http://www.athenasmi.org/resources/case-studies/the-edge-office-building/.

Beatley, Timothy. 2000. *Green Urbanism: Learning from European Cities.* Washington, DC: Island Press.

———. 2004. *Native to Nowhere: Sustaining Home and Community in a Global Age.* Washington, DC: Island Press.

Bose, Sudip. 2010. The height of sustainability. *Preservation* 62(2)(March/ April):20–27.

Brand, Stewart. 1994. *How Buildings Learn: What Happens after They're Built*. New York: Viking.

Breen, Ann, and Dick Rigby. 2004. *Intown Living: A Different American Dream*. Washington, DC: Island Press.

Building Research Establishment Environmental Assessment Method (BREEAM). 2011. BREEAM: The world's leading design and assessment method for sustainable buildings. Accessed November 26, 2011, http://www.breeam.org/page .jsp?id=66.

Byrne, John. 2010. National Register of Historic Places. Accessed November 27, 2011, http://nrhp.focus.nps.gov/natreg/docs/All_Data.html.

Campagna, Barbara A. 2008. How changes to LEED™ will benefit existing and historic buildings. *Forum News* XV(2)(November/December):1–2, 6. Accessed November 26, 2011, http://www.preservationnation.org/magazine/2009/march -april/Forum_News-Campagna.pdf.

CanadianArchitect.com. n.d. Measures of sustainability. Accessed on November 26, 2011, http://www.canadianarchitect.com/asf/perspectives_sustainibility/measures _of_sustainablity/measures_of_sustainability_embodied.htm.

Carroon, Jean. 2010. *Sustainable Preservation: Greening Existing Buildings*. Hoboken, NJ: Wiley.

Center for Business and Economic Research (CBER). 2009. Cultural tourism in Indiana: The impact and clustering of the arts and creative activities in this recession. Accessed November 26, 2011, http://cber.iweb.bsu.edu/research/ CulturalTourism.pdf.

Christman Company. 2011. The Christman Building LEED CS and LEED CI: A case study. Accessed December 4, 2011, http://www.christmanco.com/images/ ChristmanBuilding_CaseStudy.pdf.

Cockram, Michael. 2005. Reusability by design. *Architecture Week*, August 17, 2005:B1.1–2. Accessed July 2, 2010, http://www.architectureweek.com/2005/0817/ building_1-2.html.

Courts.mo.gov. 2011. The St. Louis Old Post Office and Custom House. Accessed December 4, 2011, http://www.courts.mo.gov/page.jsp?id=3502.

Cross, Gary. 2000. *An All-Consuming Century: Why Commercialism Won in Modern America*. New York: Columbia University Press.

Crowhurst Lennard, Suzanne, and Henry Lennard. 1995. *Livable Cities Observed: A Source Book of Images and Ideas*. Carmel, CA: Gondolier.

Croxton Collaborative. 1994. *Audubon House: Building the Environmentally Responsible, Energy-Efficient Office*. New York: Wiley.

Culturalheritagetourism.org. 2011. Getting started: How to succeed in cultural

heritage tourism. Accessed February 26, 2012, http://www.culturalheritagetourism
.org/howtogetstarted.htm.

Curtis, Wayne. 2002. No clear solution. *Preservation* 54(5)(September/October):
46–51, 118.

———. 2008. A cautionary tale: Amid our green building boom, why neglecting the
old in favor of the new just might cost us dearly. *Preservation*, January/February.
Accessed July 2, 2010, http://www.preservationnation.org/magazine/2008/january
-february/cautionary-tale.html.

Daly, Herman E., and Kenneth N. Townsend. 1993. *Valuing the Earth: Economics,
Ecology, Ethics*. Cambridge, MA: MIT Press.

DeCourcy Hinds, Michael. 1986. Baltimore is the model of success in urban
homesteading. *Chicago Tribune*, February 2. Accessed June 7, 2010, http://articles
.chicagotribune.com/1986-02-02/news/8601090173_1_homesteading-program
-rehab-express-crisis-in-affordable-housing/2.

Department of the Treasury/Internal Revenue Service. 2002. Market Segment
Specialization Program (MSSP): Rehabilitation tax credit. Accessed July 14, 2010,
http://www.irs.gov/pub/irs-mssp/rehab.pdf.

Dono, Andrea L. 2010. Save America's Treasures needs some saving of its own.
National Main Street Center website. Accessed July 26, 2010, http://www
.preservationnation.org/main-street/main-street-news/story-of-the-week/2010/
save-americas-treasures.html.

Dwight, Pamela, ed. 1993. *Landmark Yellow Pages*. Washington, DC: National Trust
for Historic Preservation.

Earth Advantage Institute. 2011. Top ten green trends for 2011. Accessed August
7, 2011, http://www.earthadvantage.org/resources/press-room/press-releases/
top-ten-green-building-trends-for-2011/.

EcoCity Builders. 2010. The problem. Accessed February 20, 2012, http://www
.ecocitybuilders.org/why-ecocities/the-problem-2/.

Edwards, Andres R. 2005. *The Sustainability Revolution*. Gabriola Island, BC:
New Society.

Elefante, Carl. 2007. The greenest building is . . . one that is already built. *Forum
Journal* 23(4)(Summer):26–38. Accessed January 13, 2008, http://www.
preservationnation.org/issues/sustainability/additionalresources/Forum_Journal
_Summer2007_Elifante.pdf.

Elkington, John. 1998. *Cannibals with Forks: The Triple Bottom Line of 21st Century
Business*. Gabriola Island, BC: New Society.

Enterprise Community Investment. 2006. About [the LIHTC program]. Accessed
July 16, 2010, http://www.enterprisecommunity.com/about/history.asp.

Fine, Adrian, and Jim Lindberg. 2002. *Protecting America's Historic Neighborhoods: Taming the Teardown Trend*. Washington, DC: National Trust for Historic Preservation.

Fitch, James Marston. 1990. *Historic Preservation: Curatorial Management of the Built World*. Charlottesville: University of Virginia Press.

Friedman, Thomas L. 2009. *Hot, Flat, and Crowded: Why We Need a Green Revolution—and How It Can Renew America*. New York: Picador.

Gardi, Gavin. 2011. Civic commitment. *High Performing Buildings*, Summer. Accessed December 5, 2011, http://www.hpbmagazine.org/images/stories/articles/Christman.pdf.

GlassSteelandStone.com. 2011. Old Post Office (as described by the U.S. General Services Administration). Accessed December 3, 2011, http://www.glasssteelandstone.com/BuildingDetail/1610.php.

Gratz, Roberta Brandes. 2010. *The Battle for Gotham: New York in the Shadow of Robert Moses and Jane Jacobs*. New York: Nation Books.

Green Building Initiative. 2011. Green Globes. Accessed November 26, 2011, http://www.thegbi.org/green-globes/.

Grimmer, Anne E., Jo Ellen Hensley, Liz Petrella, and Audrey T. Tepper. 2011. *The Secretary of the Interior's Standards for Rehabilitation & Illustrated Guidelines on Sustainability for Rehabilitating Historic Buildings*. Washington, DC: National Trust for Historic Preservation. Accessed August 20, 2011, http://www.nps.gov/history/hps/tps/download/guidelines-sustainability.pdf.

Habitat for Humanity. 2012. ReStore resale outlets. Accessed February 27, 2012, http://www.habitat.org/restores/.

Heschong Mahone Group. 2011. Daylighting and productivity—CEC PIER: Executive summaries. Accessed November 25, 2011, http://h-m-g.com/projects/daylighting/summaries%20on%20daylighting.htm#Windows and Offices: A Study of Office Worker Performance and the Indoor Environment - CEC PIER 2003.

HUD-DOT-EPA. 2011. Partnership for Sustainable Communities. Accessed November 27, 2011, http://www.sustainablecommunities.gov/.

Hykan, Wayne H. 2009. *Combining the New Market Tax Credit with Rehabilitation Tax Credit and the Energy Tax Credits*. An Arizona Alliance Training Session, November 18, 2009. Accessed July 15, 2010, http://azhousingalliance.org/yahoo_site_admin/assets/docs/NMTCRehabEnergy_Tax_Credits.322115639.PPT.

Institute for Local Self-Reliance (ILSR). n.d. The New Rules Project: Recycling and solid waste. Accessed June 29, 2010, http://www.newrules.org/environment/rules/recycling-and-solid-waste.

Internal Revenue Service. 2011. Rehabilitation tax credit recapture. Accessed
    November 24, 2011, http://www.irs.gov/pub/irs-utl/tax_credit_recapture_brief
    .pdf.

International Centre for the Study of the Preservation and Restoration of Cultural
    Property (ICCROM). 2011. Brief history. Accessed July 9, 2011, http://www
    .iccrom.org/eng/00about_en/00_03history_en.shtml.

International Codes Council. 2011. International Green Construction Code.
    Accessed August 10, 2011, http://www.iccsafe.org/cs/IGCC/Pages/default.aspx.

International Congress of Monuments and Sites (ICOMOS). n.d.-a. Athens Charter
    of 1931. Accessed July 5, 2011, http://www.icomos.org/athens_charter.html.

———. n.d.-b. Venice Charter of 1964. Accessed July 5, 2011, http://www.icomos
    .org/venice_charter.html#conservation.

Jackson, Mike. 2005. Embodied energy and historic preservation: A needed
    reassessment. *APT Bulletin* 38(4):45–52.

Jakle, John A., and David Wilson. 1992. *Derelict Landscapes: The Wasting of
    America's Built Environment*. Savage, MD: Rowman & Littlefield.

Jester, Thomas C., and Sharon C. Park. 1993. *Making Historic Properties Accessible*.
    Preservation brief no. 32. Washington, DC: Government Printing Office, US
    Department of the Interior.

Jokilehto, Jukka. 1999. *A History of Architectural Conservation*. Oxford, UK:
    Butterworth Heinemann.

Joss, Simon. 2009. *Eco-Cities: A Global Survey 2009*. Accessed August 3, 2011,
    http://www.westminster.ac.uk/__data/assets/pdf_file/0006/57966/Eco-Cities
    -Survey-2009-Joss.pdf.

Kienle, James T. 2008. That old building may be the greenest on the block.
    AIArchitect This Week. Accessed March 23, 2010, http://info.aia.org/aiarchitect/
    thisweek08/0208/0208p_pres.cfm.

Kiviat, Barbara. 2009. Reinventing the McMansion. *Time*. 174(12):57–58.

Kromer, John. 2010. *Fixing Broken Cities: The Implementation of Urban
    Development Strategies*. New York: Routledge.

Levitt, Julia. 2010. Preservation and sustainability: The district approach. *Metropolis*,
    September 22. Accessed August 7, 2011, http://www.metropolismag.com/
    pov/20100922/preservation-and-sustainability-the-district-approach.

Listokin, David, and Michael L. Lahr. 2011. *Second Annual Report on the Economic
    Impact of the Federal Historic Tax Credit*. Rutgers, NJ: Edward J. Bloustein
    School of Planning and Public Policy. Accessed November 10, 2011, http://www.
    preservationnation.org/issues/community-revitalization/jobs/2nd_Annual
    _Rutgers_Report.pdf.

Lord, Noelle. 2007. Embracing efficiency. *Old House Journal* 35(5)(September/ October):40–45.

Lowenthal, David. 2005. Stewarding the future. *CRM: The Journal of Heritage Stewardship* 2(2 Summer 2005):20–39.

Lyon, Elizabeth. 1993. Historic preservation and successful communities: A strategy for economic and community development. *Forum Journal* 7(5)(September/ October 1993). Accessed July 24, 2010, http://www.preservationnation.org/forum/ resource-center/forum-library/members-only/historic-preservation-and -successful-communities.html.

McInnis, Maggie, and Ilene R. Tyler. 2005. The greening of the Samuel T. Dana building: A classroom and laboratory for sustainable design. *APT Bulletin* 36(4):39–45.

Michigan Municipal League. 2010. Christman headquarters becomes world's first Triple Platinum LEED certified building. Accessed December 4, 2011, http:// www.mml.org/newsroom/press_releases/2010_11_8_christman-leed.html.

Miller, Julia. 2004. *Protecting Older Neighborhoods Through Conservation District Programs*. Washington, DC: National Trust for Historic Preservation.

Mize, Jeffrey. 2009. Historic preservation a key component of downtown revitalization: Business expert decries demolishing older buildings for so-called green construction. Accessed November 10, 2009, http://www.allbusiness.com/ environment-natural-resources/pollution-monitoring/12430961-1.html.

Moe, Richard. 2007. President's report: Opening plenary. NTHP website. Accessed November 1, 2009, http://www.preservationnation.org/about-us/press-center/soe/ speeches/presidents-report-2007.html.

———. 2008. *Sustainability and Historic Preservation*. Speech presented at the Los Angeles Conservancy November 12, 2008. Accessed May 12, 2009, http://www .preservationnation.org/about-us/press-center/soe/speeches/sustainability-and -historic.html.

Morton, W. Brown III, Gary L. Hume, Kay D. Weeks, and H. Ward Jandl. 1992. *The Secretary of the Interior's Standards for Rehabilitation and Illustrated Guidelines for Rehabilitating Historic Buildings*. Washington, DC: US Department of the Interior.

Murtagh, James W. 2006. *Keeping Time: The History and Theory of Preservation in America*, 3rd ed. Hoboken, NJ: Wiley.

National Conference of State Historic Preservation Officers (NCSHPO). 2010. Historic preservation: A significant source of local jobs. Accessed June 3, 2010, http://www.ncshpo.org/current/legislation/2010%201-pagers/20100318Jobs.pdf.

National Main Street Center (NMSC). 2010a. The eight principles. Accessed May

31, 2010, http://www.preservationnation.org/main-street/about-main-street/the
-approach/eight-principles.html.

———. 2010b. History of the National Trust Main Street Center. Accessed May 31,
2010, http://www.preservationnation.org/main-street/about-main-street/the-center/
history.html#transition.

———. 2010c. Main Street program. Accessed May 31, 2010, http://www.preserva
tionnation.org/main-street/about-main-street/the-programs/.

———. 2010d. What happened to Main Street. Accessed May 31, 2010, http://www
.preservationnation.org/main-street/about-main-street/getting-started/what
-happened-to-main-street.html.

National Park Service (NPS). 2009. Historic preservation tax incentives.
Washington, DC: National Park Service. Accessed November 24, 2011, http://
www.nps.gov/history/hps/tps/tax/download/HPTI_brochure.pdf.

———. 2010a. Federal tax incentives for rehabilitating historic buildings: Statistical
report and analysis for fiscal year 2009. Washington, DC: National Park Service.
Accessed July 12, 2010, http://www.nps.gov/history/hps/TPS/tax/download/
annual_report_09.pdf.

———. 2010b. Frequently asked questions [about CLG grants]. Accessed November
24, 2011, http://www.nps.gov/history/HPS/clg/faqs.html#2.

———. 2010c. Save America's Treasures program detail. Accessed July 23, 2010,
http://www.nps.gov/history/hps/treasures/ProgramDetails.htm.

———. 2011a. National Heritage Areas. Accessed November 26, 2011, http://www
.nps.gov/history/heritageareas/FAQ/.

———. 2011b. National Register of Historic Places. Accessed November 27, 2011,
http://www.nps.gov/nr/.

———. 2011c. Show me the money: Tapping federal funds for historic preservation.
Accessed November 24, 2011, http://www.nps.gov/hps/hpg/downloads/Show
-Me-the-Money-Oct2011.pdf.

———. 2011d. The treatment of historic properties. Accessed July 27, 2011, http://
www2.cr.nps.gov/tps/standards.htm.

National Trust Community Investment Corporation (NTCIC). 2005. Investments
by the National Trust Community Investment Corporation. Accessed July 17,
2010, http://www.ntcicfunds.com/library/NTCIC_portfolio.pdf.

———. 2011. Old Post Office, St. Louis MO. Accessed December 3, 2011, http://
ntcicfunds.com/projects/old-post-office-st-louis-mo/.

National Trust for Historic Preservation (NTHP). 1983. *With Heritage So Rich*.
Washington, DC: Preservation Press.

———. 2008. Pocantico proclamation on sustainability and historic preservation.

Accessed July 27, 2011, http://www.preservationnation.org/issues/sustainability/
additional-resources/Pocantico-Proclamation.pdf.

———. 2009. Historic wood windows. Accessed July 2, 2010, http://www.preserva
tionnation.org/about-us/regional-offices/northeast/additional-resources/2009
-Revised-Window-Tip-Sheet-1.pdf.

———. 2010a. History. Accessed May 23, 2010, http://www.preservationnation.org/
about-us/history.html.

———. 2010b. Preservation Green Lab. Accessed July 29, 2010, http://www
.preservationnation.org/issues/sustainability/green-lab/.

———. 2010c. Save America's Treasures. Accessed July 23, 2010, http://www
.preservationnation.org/travel-and-sites/save-americas-treasures/about.html.

———. 2011a. About the Preservation Green Lab. Accessed August 3, 2011, http://
www.preservationnation.org/issues/sustainability/green-lab/about.html.

———. 2011b. Liz Dunn. Accessed August 7, 2011, http://www.preservationnation.
org/issues/sustainability/green-lab/profiles/liz-dunn.html.

———. 2011c. Policy innovation. Accessed August 7, 2011, http://www
.preservationnation.org/issues/sustainability/green-lab/policy-innovation.html.

Nelson, Arthur C. 2011. *What Americans Want*. Public presentation at 101112 Speaker
Series sponsored by the University of Utah College of Architecture + Planning,
Salt Lake City, Utah, November 3, 2011.

New York State Office of Parks, Recreation & Historic Preservation. 2011. Certified
Local Government program. Accessed November 24, 2011, http://nysparks.state
.ny.us/grants/certified-local-government/default.aspx.

NJN Public Television and Radio. 2009. *Green Builders* [DVD]. Trenton, NJ:
NJN Public Television and Radio. Accessed July 3, 2010, http://www.pbs.org/
greenbuilders/watch-the-film.html.

Office of Historic Preservation. 2011. Certified local government program. Accessed
November 24, 2011, http://ohp.parks.ca.gov/?page_id=21239.

O'Neill, David. 1999. *Smart Growth: Myth and Fact*. Washington, DC: The Urban
Land Institute.

Osdoba, Tom, and Liz Dunn. 2010. The role of district energy in greening existing
neighborhoods. Accessed February 20, 2012, http://www.preservationnation.org/
issues/sustainability/green-lab/additional-resources/District-Energy-Summary.pdf.

Owen, David. 2009. *Green Metropolis: Why Living Small, Living Closer, and
Driving Less Are the Keys to Sustainability*. London: Penguin.

Pavao, William. 2011. A description of California Tax Credit Allocation Committee
programs. Accessed November 24, 2011, http://www.treasurer.ca.gov/ctcac/
program.pdf.

Porter, Douglas R. 2002. *Making Smart Growth Work*. Washington, DC: Urban Land Institute.

Portland Sustainability Institute. 2012. Ecodistricts. Accessed February 20, 2012, http://www.pdxinstitute.org/index.php/ecodistricts.

Preservation Green Lab. 2012. The greenest building: Quantifying the environ mental value of building reuse. Accessed February 27, 2012, http://www .preservationnation.org/issues/sustainability/green-lab/lca/The_Greenest_ Building_lowres.pdf.

Racer, Anne. 2002. University student housing at Fort Douglas. Script for speech presented at the Fort Douglas 140th anniversary commemoration, Salt Lake City, UT.

Register, Richard. 2006. *Ecocities: Rebuilding Cities in Balance with Nature*. Gabriola Island, BC: New Society.

Richardson, Margaret Milner. 2011. PS3993. Accessed October 5, 2011, http://www .irs.gov/pub/irs-regs/ps3993.txt.

Roberts, Tristan. 2007. Historic preservation and green building: A lasting relationship. *Environmental Building News* 16(1). Accessed February 27, 2012, http://www.buildinggreen.com/auth/article.cfm/2007/1/2/ Historic-Preservation-and-Green-Building-A-Lasting-Relationship/.

Rypkema, Donovan D. 2002a. The (economic) value of National Register listing. *Cultural Resource Management* 25(1):6–7. Accessed October 6, 2011, http://crm .cr.nps.gov/issue.cfm?volume=25&number=01.

———. 2002b. *A Guide to Tax-Advantaged Rehabilitation*. Washington, DC: National Trust for Historic Preservation.

———. 2005. *The Economics of Historic Preservation: A Community Leader's Guide*. Washington, DC: National Trust for Historic Preservation.

———. 2006. Economics, sustainability, and historic preservation. *Forum Journal* 20(2). Accessed February 21, 2009, http://forum.nationaltrust.org/subNTHP/ displayNews.asp?lib_ID=921.

———. 2007a. *Historic, Green and Profitable*. Speech to the Traditional Building Conference, March 8, 2007. Accessed June 12, 2010, http://www.ptvermont.org/ rypkema_boston.htm.

———. 2007b. *Sustainability, Smart Growth and Historic Preservation*. Presented at the Historic Districts Council Annual Conference in New York City, on March 10, 2007. Accessed August 6, 2011, http://www.preservation.org/rypkema.htm.

———. 2008. Heritage conservation and the local economy. *Global Urban Development* 4(1)(August). Accessed October 10, 2009, http://www.globalurban .org/GUDMag08Vol4Iss1/Rypkema.htm#_edn13.

————. 2010. Save America's Treasures update. *PlaceEconomics Blog*. Accessed February 11, 2010, http://www.placeeconomics.com/2010/02/save-americas-treasures-update.html.

St. Louis' US Custom House & Post Office Building Associates, LLP. 2011. The Old Post Office: St. Louis. Accessed December 3, 2011, http://www.oldpostofficestl.com/.

Salt Lake City. 2009. Salt Lake City preservation plan. Accessed June 30, 2009, http://www.slcgov.com/Council/CED/HPPlan_June09reviseddraft.pdf.

Sander, Thomas H. 2002. Social capital and new urbanism: Leading a civic horse to water. *National Civic Review* 91(3, Fall). Accessed November 25, 2011, http://www.ncl.org/publications/ncr/91-3/ncr91-3_chapter2.pdf.

Sandiegotraveltips.com. 2011. San Diego architecture near PETCO Park worth its mettle. Accessed August 1, 2011, http://www.sandiegotraveltips.com/public/San_Diego_Architecture_Near_Petco_Park_Worth_Its_Mettle.cfm.

Save Our Heritage Organisation. 2011. The greenest of conservation solutions. Accessed August 1, 2011, http://sohosandiego.org/main/greenest.htm.

Semes, Steven W. 2009. *The Future of the Past: A Conservation Ethic for Architecture, Urbanism, and Historic Preservation*. New York: W. W. Norton.

Shapiro, Shari. 2007. *Losing the Forest to Save a Few Trees: Problems behind Green Sprawl*. http://www.greenbiz.com/blog/2007/09/05/losing-forest-save-few-trees-problems-behind-green-sprawl.

Shaw, Jane S., and Ronald D. Utt, eds. 2000. *A Guide to Smart Growth: Shattering Myths, Providing Solutions*. Washington, DC: The Heritage Foundation.

Sierra Club. 1999. *Solving Sprawl*. Washington, DC: Sierra Club.

SmartGrowth.org. 2010. Principles of smart growth. Accessed May 24, 2010, http://www.smartgrowth.org/about/principles/default.asp.

Smith, Neil. 1996. *The New Urban Frontier: Gentrification and the Revanchist City*. New York: Routledge.

Solomon, Christopher. 2009. The swelling McMansion backlash. Accessed May 24, 2010, http://realestate.msn.com/article.aspx?cp-documentid=13107733.

Stein, Benjamin, John Reynolds, Walter Grondzik, and Alison Kwok. 2010. *Mechanical and Electrical Equipment for Buildings*, 11th ed. Hoboken, NJ: Wiley.

Stipe, Richard. 2003. *A Richer Heritage: Historic Preservation in the Twenty-First Century*. Chapel Hill: The University of North Carolina Press.

Stubbs, John H. 2009. *Time Honored: A Global View of Architectural Conservation*. Hoboken, NJ: Wiley.

Stubbs, John H., and Emily G. Makas. 2011. *Architectural Conservation in Europe and the Americas*. Hoboken, NJ: Wiley.

Sustainable Communities. 2010. Why buy locally. Accessed July 26, 2010, http://
sustainableconnections.org/thinklocal/why.

Taylor-Wells, Gisele. 2008. *The Greening of Historic Places: Finding Common
Ground between Historic Tax Credits and LEED Certification*. Master's thesis,
University of North Carolina Greensboro. Accessed June 17, 2010, http://libres
.uncg.edu/ir/uncg/f/umi-uncg-1574.pdf.

Tess, John M. 2010. Historic preservation and going green. *Journal of Tax Credits*
1(IV)(April). Accessed July 14, 2010, http://www.novoco.com/journal/2010/04/
news_htc_201004.php.

Texas Historical Commission. 2007. *Heritage Tourism Guidebook*. (Data cited from
Travel Industry of America Tourism Works for America 2002). Accessed July 26,
2010, http://www.thc.state.tx.us/publications/booklets/HTGuidebook.pdf.

Travel-Industry-Dictionary.com. 2011. Cultural tourist. Accessed November 26, 2011,
http://www.travel-industry-dictionary.com/cultural-tourism.html.

Trusty, Wayne. 2003. *Renovating vs. Building New: The Environmental Merits*.
Merrickville, ON: The Athena Institute, Canada. Accessed June 18, 2010, http://
www.athenasmi.org/publications/docs/OECD_paper.pdf.

Tyler, Norman, Ted J. Ligibel, and Ilene R. Tyler. 2009. *Historic Preservation:
An Introduction to Its History, Principles and Practice*, 2nd ed. New York:
W. W. Norton.

United Nations Educational, Scientific and Cultural Organization (UNESCO).
2011a. The organization's history. Accessed July 5, 2011, http://www.unesco.org/
new/en/unesco/about-us/who-we-are/history/.

———. 2011b. United States of America. Accessed July 5, 2011, http://www.unesco
.org/new/en/unesco/.

United States Department of Energy (USDOE). 2008. Commercial building energy
consumption survey, 2003. Accessed May 11, 2009, http://www.eia.doe.gov/emeu/
cbecs/cbecs2003/detailed_tables_2003/2003set19/2003pdf/e1-e11.pdf.

———. 2009. Monitoring plan for weatherization assistance program, state energy
program, energy efficiency and conservation block grants. Accessed July 20, 2010,
http://www1.eere.energy.gov/wip/pdfs/monitoring_plan.pdf.

———.2010a. Energy Efficiency and Conservation Block Grant Program. Accessed
July 20, 2010, http://www1.eere.energy.gov/wip/eecbg.html.

———. 2010b. Energy Policy Act of 1992. Accessed May 12, 2010, http://www1.eere
.energy.gov/femp/regulations/epact1992.html.

United States Department of Housing and Urban Development (HUD). 2009.
Community Development Block Grant program: Preserving America. Accessed
May 12, 2010, http://www.hud.gov/offices/cpd/communitydevelopment/library/
historicpreservation/historicpreservation.doc.

———. 2010a. Calculating housing tax credits. Accessed July 16, 2010, http://www .hud.gov/offices/cpd/affordablehousing/training/web/lihtc/calculating/.

———. 2010b. Community Development Block Grants. Accessed May 26, 2010, http://www.hud.gov/offices/adm/about/admguide/history.cfm.

———. 2010c. How housing tax credits work. Accessed July 16, 2010, http://www .hud.gov/offices/cpd/affordablehousing/training/web/lihtc/basics/work.cfm.

———. 2010d. HUD historical background. Accessed May 26, 2010, http://www .hud.gov/offices/adm/about/admguide/history.cfm.

United States Energy Information Administration (USEIA). 2010. Residential energy consumption survey. Accessed July 2, 2010, http://www.eia.doe.gov/emeu/ recs/historicaldata/total/total_pdf/total2001.pdf.

United States Environmental Protection Agency–United States Department of Energy (USEPA-USDOE). 2011. Energy Star. Accessed November 26, 2011, http://www.energystar.gov/.

United States Green Building Council (USGBC). 2010. LEED. Accessed May 12, 2010, http://www.usgbc.org/DisplayPage.aspx?CategoryID=19.

United States Office of Management and Budget. 2011. Budget of the United States government: Browse fiscal year 2011. Accessed November 24, 2011, http://www .gpoaccess.gov/usbudget/fy11/pdf/budget/housing.pdf.

United States Travel Association. 2010. Travel facts. Accessed July 26, 2010, http://www.ustravel.org/marketing/national-travel-and-tourism-week/ talking-points-and-facts.

United States Treasury (USTREAS). 2009. American Recovery and Reinvestment Act program plan: New Markets Tax Credit (NMTC) program. Accessed November 24, 2011, http://www.ustreas.gov/recovery/docs/Updated%20 ARRA%20Program%20Plan%20NMTC%20Program%205%2012%202010.pdf.

———. 2010a. Community Development Financial Institutions Fund: Recovery Act and 2009 New Markets Tax Credits program allocations. Accessed July 17, 2010, http://www.cdfifund.gov/docs/2009/nmtc/2009%20NMTC%20Program%20 Allocation%20Booklet.pdf.

———. 2010b. NMTC fact sheet. Accessed July 17, 2010, http://www.cdfifund.gov/ docs/nmtc/2010/nmtc-fact-sheetFINAL.pdf.

Utah Heritage Foundation. 2011. Preservation awards. Accessed December 3, 2011, http://www.utahheritagefoundation.com/saving-places/heritage-awards.

Whole Building Design Guide (WBDG). 2010a. Accommodate life safety and security needs. *Whole Building Design Guide*. Accessed February 26, 2012, http:// www.wbdg.org/design/accommodate_needs.php.

———. 2010b. Sustainable historic preservation. *Whole Building Design Guide*. Accessed February 26, 2012, http://www.wbdg.org/resources/sustainable_hp.php.

Winter, Noré V. 2011. *Developing Sustainability Guidelines for Historic Districts.* Washington, DC: National Trust for Historic Preservation.

Wolf, Michael Allan. 2008. *The Zoning of America: Euclid v. Ambler.* Lawrence: University Press of Kansas.

World Commission on Environment and Development (WCED). 1987. *Our Common Future.* New York: Oxford University Press.

Young, Robert A. 1998. *Reference Guide for Army Adaptive Reuse Projects.* Final draft.

———. 2004a. Fort Stephen A. Douglas: Adaptive re-use for a community of scholars. In *Protecting Our Diverse Heritage: The Role of Parks, Protected Areas, and Cultural Sites,* edited by David Harmon, Bruce M. Kilgore, and Gay E. Vietzke, 205–9. Hancock, MI: The George Wright Society.

———. 2004b. Stewardship of the built environment: The emerging synergies from sustainability and historic preservation. In *Archipelagos: Outposts of the Americas Enclaves amidst Technology,* edited by Robert Alexander Gonzalez and Marilys Rebeca Nepomechie, 35–50. Washington, DC: Association of Collegiate Schools of Architecture.

———. 2008a. *Historic Preservation Technology.* Hoboken, NJ: Wiley.

———. 2008b. Stewardship of the built environment. In *Writing Urbanism: A Design Reader,* edited by Douglas S. Kelbaugh and Kit McCullough, 57–60. New York: Routledge.

———. 2008c. Striking gold: Historic preservation and LEED. *Journal of Green Building* 3(1)(Winter):24–43.

Index